# GERALDINE ROCKEFELLER DODGE

BY BARBARA J. MITNICK

A publication of the
Geraldine R. Dodge Foundation
Morristown, New Jersey
2000

Geraldine R. Dodge Foundation
163 Madison Avenue
Morristown, New Jersey 07962-1239



ISBN 0-9704217-0-2 (hardbound)
0-9704217-1-0 (soft cover)

Library of Congress Number 00-107664

Editors: Phil Freshman, Ari Korpivaara
Designer: Bethany Johns
Indexers: Eileen Quam, Barbara J. Mitnick
Additional Photography: Timothy W. Volk
Printer: Meridian Printing

Front cover and page 6
Friedrich August von Kaulbach (German, 1850–1920)
*Geraldine Rockefeller*, 1906
Oil on canvas, 33 ¹/₂ x 30 in.
(Courtesy of The Morris Museum, Morristown, New Jersey)

Back cover and page 122
Photograph of Geraldine Rockefeller Dodge,
about 1940
(Courtesy of the Geraldine R. Dodge Foundation)

# CONTENTS

GERALDINE ROCKEFELLER DODGE FAMILY TREE

Godfrey Rockefeller
1783–1857

Lucy Avery
1786–1867

William Avery Rockefeller
1810–1906

John Davison
1773–1858

Cynthia Selover
1776–1823

Eliza Davison
1813–1889

Joel Goodsell
1775–1834

Mary Kirtland
1774–1840

David Judson Goodsell, Sr.
1804–1889

William O'Brien
?–after 1832

Mary Ann
Cunningham
1768–1856

Ellen O'Brien
1809–1855

Lucy Rockefeller
1838–1878

John Davison Rockefeller
1839–1937

**William Rockefeller**
**1841–1922**

Mary Ann Rockefeller
1843–1925

Franklin Rockefeller
1845–1917

Frances Rockefeller
1845–1847

Esther Judson Goodsell
1828–1908

Mary Elizabeth Goodsell
1830–1902

Sarah Ann Goodsell
1830–1906

Ellen Louisa Goodsell
1832–1900

David Judson Goodsell, Jr.
1834–1863

Lewis Wheeler Goodsell
1837–1838

Charles Henry Goodsell
1839–1878

Jeremiah Denison Goodsell
1841–1847

**Almira Geraldine Goodsell**
**1844–1920**

John Lewis Goodsell
1846–1847

Amelia Frances Goodsell
1855–1855

Louis Edward Rockefeller
1865–1866

Emma Rockefeller
1868–1934

William Goodsell Rockefeller
1870–1922

John Davison Rockefeller II
1872–1877

Percy Avery Rockefeller
1878–1934

**Ethel Geraldine Rockefeller**
**1882–1973**

(m. Marcellus Hartley Dodge 1907)

Marcellus Hartley Dodge, Jr.
1908–1930

Friedrich August von Kaulbach
Portrait of Geraldine Rockefeller, 1906

# PREFACE AND ACKNOWLEDGMENTS

On a rainy day in the fall of 1975, a friend and I stood on a long
line, waiting to view the contents of Giralda Farms, the estate of
Geraldine Rockefeller Dodge. Like Mrs. Dodge, we were residents
of Madison, New Jersey. However, largely because of her age and
declining state of health, we had never had the opportunity to
meet her. Hidden from the road, her home was the subject of
local legend. We knew of her generosity to Madison, her interest
in animals and their welfare, and the loss of her only child—a
son in whose memory she built and donated to Madison a magnificent borough hall. We understood much less about her life
and the extraordinary magnitude of her interests.

She had died two years earlier. After St. Hubert's Giralda,
the animal welfare organization she founded in 1939, and the
Geraldine R. Dodge Foundation, established in her will, received
some of the artwork, the Fidelity Union Trust Company (the
executor of her last will) had consigned the rest of the contents
of her estate to be catalogued and sold at auction by New York's
Sotheby Parke Bernet. Billed as the largest on-site sale ever held
by Sotheby's, the event at Giralda Farms seemed to be just that.
From her everyday attire and the ordinary furnishings of her
kitchen and workrooms to her most valuable jewelry, exquisite
American and Continental furniture, paintings, and bronzes, the
accumulation of a lifetime was on the market. My friend and I
wanted to own something to remind us of Mrs. Dodge, so she
purchased a set of carved-stone bookends from the accompanying tag sale, and I, the budding art historian, became the proud
owner of a copy of Wilhelm Lubke's two-volume *Outlines of the
History of Art* (1879).

It has been a quarter-century since that rainy day, and
Geraldine Rockefeller Dodge, through the foundation created in
her name, has had an important and positive impact on animal
welfare, on education, on the arts, and, indeed, on my career
as an independent curator. In 1992 the Geraldine R. Dodge
Foundation underwrote my retrospective exhibition of the
works of the preeminent New Jersey painter Adolf Konrad
(b. 1915). Six years later, when I received a phone call from the
Foundation's then-executive director, Scott McVay, asking if I
would consider writing a biography of Mrs. Dodge, I was
immediately intrigued—and I readily accepted. Questions soon
began filling my mind: Which Rockefeller was she? How did she
develop her interests? What had led her to acquire a large and
varied art collection? What was behind her establishment of
a foundation that now ranks among the major organizations of
its kind in the United States? As I embarked on my research,
friends and family began asking about her. During many an
evening at the dinner table, the conversation revolved around
Mrs. Dodge and my latest discovery. One of the most delightfully
astonishing of these came when, as I was reading her diaries
at the Rockefeller Archive Center, I learned that more than a
century ago she had been a guest in my home, then owned by
the family of one of her closest friends, Louise Scribner!

Researching and writing this book has been a most rewarding
experience, in part because it has provided me with a chance
to clear up the many misconceptions about Mrs. Dodge that
surfaced both during her lifetime and after her death. For giving
me these opportunities, I will always be grateful to Scott McVay
and to Robert LeBuhn, president of the Geraldine R. Dodge
Foundation Board of Trustees. Throughout the project, the staff
of the Foundation was enormously helpful, especially David
Grant, the present executive director, John Yingling, Susan
Pilshaw, Cynthia Evans, Vera DuMont, and George A. Aguilar,
the Foundation's attorney.

Various organizations and individuals also contributed time
and information. I was most fortunate to be able to interview

Mary Jane Ellis—Mrs. Dodge's trusted friend and companion during her later years—who traveled to Morristown from her home in Massachusetts to provide wonderful recollections; Helen Hartley Mead Platt and Nicolas W. Platt, particularly with regard to the life and career of Marcellus Hartley Dodge; and, representing the Rockefeller family, O. Stillman Rockefeller and Christopher J. Elliman. I am grateful to Michele Hiltzik, Thomas Rosenbaum, and the staff of the Rockefeller Archive Center in North Tarrytown, New York, for making the William Rockefeller family papers available and for introducing me to Laura and George Levy, co-authors of a forthcoming biography of William Rockefeller. The Levys were extraordinarily generous in providing genealogies of the Rockefeller and Goodsell families and sharing information and insights with regard to Rockefeller family history. Katherine Holland and Daniel J. Linke of the Alumni Records and Archives offices at Princeton University provided important assistance. Madlyn Deming, director of communications, and Michele Haberland, alumni director of the Spence School, as well as Jesse Mygatt of the Alumni Federation Office and Jocelyn Wilk and Sharon Williams of the Columbia University Archives offered useful material. Also helpful in this regard were Mary Ellen Graf and Louise Quinlan of the Morristown Memorial Hospital and Shannon Slama, museum assistant of the American Kennel Club Museum of the Dog in St. Louis, Missouri. Drs. Leland Carmichael and Douglas McGregor of the College of Veterinary Medicine at Cornell University in Ithaca, New York, and Jeanne Griffith of that school's Office of Public Affairs also supplied important information concerning Mrs. Dodge's far-reaching support for Cornell's James A. Baker Institute for Animal Health.

My thanks go as well to Nancy Warner Adamczyk, director, and Helene Corlett of the Madison Public Library; to Maria W. Fenton, president of the Madison Historical Society; to Meg Strubel, vice-president of St. Hubert's Giralda; to Ted Monica, former Madison High School football coach and athletic director; to Robert Graham, Jr., present owner of New York's James Graham Gallery; to Meg Poltorak of the Morris Museum; and to Korin

Rosenkrans and Cheryl Turkington of the Morristown/Morris Township Library's Local History Department. My thanks are also extended to Madison's present mayor, John J. Dunne, for his wonderful recollections of Geraldine Rockefeller Dodge, her family, and Giralda Farms; to James Allison, the Madison borough administrator, who took me on a most interesting tour of the Hartley Dodge Memorial; to Phil Freshman and Ari Korpivaara for their insights and editing; Bethany Johns for her layout and design; and to Jane Mitnick for her careful proofreading.

Finally, I am grateful, as always, to my husband, Howard, for keeping the home fires burning and for giving me encouragement as I worked on this wonderful project.


Barbara J. Mitnick
Morristown, New Jersey
June 2000

# CHAPTER I

# EARLY LIFE

Saturday, October 4, 1975, was the first day of the exhibition of the collections of Ethel Geraldine Rockefeller Dodge at Giralda Farms in Madison, New Jersey. A lovely landscape dotted with beautiful shrubs and rare-specimen trees led visitors to a large Elizabethan Revival house whose front door opened to reveal the remnants of a vanished way of life. Giralda was Mrs. Dodge's home from 1916 until her death in 1973, at age ninety-one. And on this day, the general public was admitted inside for the first time. Numerous items in the collection listed in a 575-page appraisal, particularly bronzes of animals and paintings of dogs, had already been given to St. Hubert's Giralda, the animal welfare organization she created in 1939. The Geraldine R. Dodge Foundation, established in her will, was to receive other artwork. In addition, a number of objects had been transported to New York City for sale in a series of Sotheby's auctions. At Giralda, the attention of the mass media, including newspapers and magazines, was on the "sale of the century." The first auction was scheduled to begin in three days, and on this first day of viewing, fifteen thousand people would arrive.[1]

For some, it was a day of remembrance. Several of Mrs. Dodge's former employees, saddened at thoughts of the end of an era, remembered her generosity and expressed a desire to protect her memory. Mary Jane Ellis, who had been her trusted aide and companion from September 1958 until three years before her death, worried about an invasion of privacy, as her most personal items were on display and about to be sold. Herbert W. Ball, an officer of Fidelity Union Trust Company (the executor of Mrs. Dodge's last will), reminisced about the complexity of running Giralda Farms, a business employing seventy-nine people at the time of her death, with a hundred animals in the kennels. He had been responsible for protecting the contents of the mansion, ten miles of estate roads, and, of course, Mrs. Dodge herself, who had been an invalid during her last years. Ernest Barton, her English butler from 1937 until she died, could still picture Mrs. Dodge ascending the stairs at the end of an evening and calling out, "Ernest, that was a wonderful dinner. Thank you very much, and goodnight." [2]

The citizens of Madison could only imagine the treasures contained in Mrs. Dodge's home. Giralda was situated near the Morris County residences of some of the wealthiest families in the nation—a counterpart of Newport, Rhode Island, with homes befitting the affluence of their occupants. One source noted that hundreds of men and women, with an aggregate wealth of almost $3 billion, lived in and around Morristown during the late nineteenth and early twentieth centuries. Indeed, Frelinghuysens, Harknesses, Kahns, Scribners, Twomblys, and Vanderbilts had hired the finest architects of that period to build extraordinary residences, some of which echoed English and French palaces and manor houses, while others evoked the Colonial American heritage. Giralda's size and grandeur suited Mrs. Dodge, for she was the daughter of one of the richest men in America, William Rockefeller, and the niece of William's better-known brother, John D. By the time she was born, the family name had become almost a generic word for great wealth, and during her lifetime it also came to signify philanthropy on an enormous scale. The combined estates of Geraldine and Marcellus Hartley Dodge had also become famous for the Morris and Essex Kennel Club Dog Show, reportedly the largest and most elaborate in the world. But prior to this day, few Madisonians were aware of the scope and quality of her collections. Also, aside from the Rockefeller name, few knew much about her origins.[3]

Ethel Geraldine Rockefeller began her life on April 3, 1882. She was thus a child of the Gilded Age, a term coined by the nineteenth-century social critic and satirist Mark Twain in *The Gilded Age* (1873). He and his co-author, Charles Dudley Warner, wrote about the fortunes being accumulated by "captains of industry"—financiers and tycoons—as a period of enormous and unprecedented commercial and industrial expansion unfolded in America. Although these developments stirred optimism and a sense of national rebirth in the wake of the Civil War, Twain and Warner, pointing to the greed and gaudy wealth of the time, characterized it as "gilded" rather than "golden." The building of the intercontinental railroads, the creation of large-scale manu-facturing and banking firms, and the rapid growth of the oil business, among other developments, had led a tremendous amount of money to be concentrated in the hands of a relatively few American families, including the Astors, Carnegies, Morgans, Rockefellers, and Vanderbilts. They viewed the earning of great sums by means of ingenuity and sustained effort as important, even noble work. According to one historian of the Gilded Age, L. Marx Renzulli, this was a marriage of Victorian morality and the old Puritan work ethic. But these affluent people also felt obliged to return some of their good fortune to the community at large. Andrew Carnegie summarized this obligation in his famous 1889 sermon, "The Gospel of Wealth," in which he identified the man of wealth as "the mere trustee and agent for his poorer brethren."[4]

The American Rockefellers trace their lineage to French and German ancestors. In 1723, Johann Peter Rockefelter (b. 1682) arrived in the American colonies with his wife and five children, establishing a farm at Amwell in Hunterdon County, New Jersey. Twelve years later, Johann's cousin Diell (b. 1695) emigrated with his family, settling in Germantown, in Albany County, New York.[5]

Johann Peter's great-grandson Godfrey Rockefeller (b. 1783) and his wife Lucy Avery (b. 1786) had a son, William Avery, who was born in 1810 in Ancrum, in Columbia County, New York. Later known as "Big Bill" and, in some circles, as "Devil Bill" or

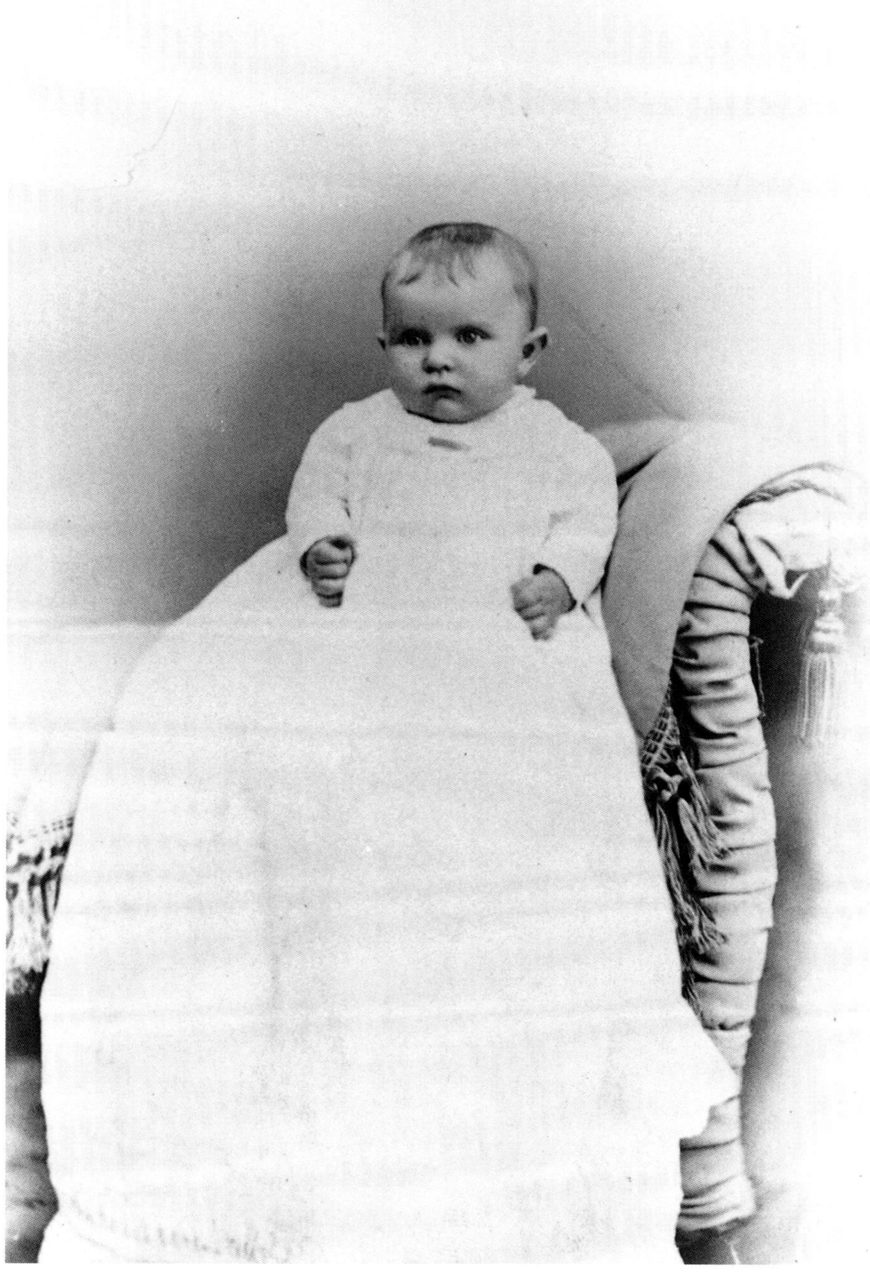

Ethel Geraldine Rockefeller, 1882
(Courtesy of St. Hubert's Giralda)

"Wild Bill," he achieved a reputation as the family's most colorful
and flamboyant member. On February 18, 1837, he married the
redheaded, blue-eyed, and attractive—but pious and retiring—
Eliza Davison, daughter of a relatively prosperous farmer, John
Davison (son of George Davison, who served and died during
the Revolutionary War), and Cynthia Selover of New Brunswick,
New Jersey. Bill's wily charm intrigued the sedate Eliza, but her
rather straitlaced father had strongly objected to the match,
suspecting that Bill's reasons for marrying his daughter had
more to do with her comfortable financial circumstances than
with romance. Indeed, the two proved to be emotionally incom-
patible. Nevertheless, they produced six children, beginning in
1838 with the birth of a daughter, Lucy. On July 8, 1839, their
first son, John Davison Rockefeller, arrived.[6]

Bill was perpetually on the move around the country, working as a salesman, confidence man, and medical quack (using the
pseudonym "Dr. William Levingston") and becoming involved in
highly questionable business and personal relationships. Eliza
stayed at home, at first in Richford, and then in Moravia, New
York, and later on a farm outside Cleveland, Ohio, tending to her
children and to her religion. From time to time Bill would return,
flush with cash, and pay his debts, but he remained a controver-
sial character all his life.[7]

Due to Bill's long and mysterious absences, it is understand-
able that the Rockefeller children were more heavily influenced
by Eliza, particularly by her self-discipline, patience, and austerity.
Throughout his life, John D., in particular, remained devoted
to his mother, to her devout Baptist faith, and to emulating her
charitable nature. Even at the outset of what was to become a
remarkable and enormously lucrative career, he regularly donated
a portion of his limited income to his church and to Baptist
missions. After the Civil War, as his wealth dramatically increased,
he expanded his philanthropy to include vocational-training institutions, orphanages, and even individuals qualifying as a result of
legitimate hard-luck stories. John D.'s wife, Laura Celestia (Cettie)
Spelman, whom he married on September 8, 1864, proved to be

This photograph of John D. Rockefeller, Sr, taken about 1924, was displayed for more than four decades on the piano at Giralda. (Courtesy of Nicolas W. Platt)

as generous and devout as her husband, holding Baptist prayer sessions with her family every morning before breakfast, isolating her children from frivolity and immoral activities, and generally eschewing the trappings of her growing prosperity.[8]

By 1863, John D. (later referred to as "Senior") had begun investing profits from his grain business in oil. Then, true to his upbringing, after he had accumulated his first fortune, he began giving away money in record amounts. By 1933, many years after his only son, John D., Jr. (known in the family as "Junior"), had been put in charge of the family's philanthropies, Rockefeller gifts reportedly totaled more than $780 million for public and private charities, institutions of learning, and other projects designed to benefit museums, housing developments, and the restoration of Colonial Williamsburg. Junior's own sons—John D. III, Nelson, Laurence, Winthrop and David—continued to support worthy charities and nonprofit organizations, largely through the Rockefeller Brothers Fund.[9]

William and Eliza's second son, William, was more lively and sociable than his older brother, reflecting the temperaments of both his mother and father. But William's personal life, unlike that of his father, was untarnished; in fact, he remained a steadfastly devoted family man. He was as hardworking as John D. but less strict in his religious practices, even to the extent of eventually abandoning the Baptist faith of his youth in favor of the Episcopal Church.

Born in Richford, New York, on May 31, 1841, William was educated first at Owego Academy, then, beginning in 1853, when the family moved to a farm near Cleveland, at that growing city's Central High School. But he never graduated, because in the spring of 1857, John D. recruited him to work under him at the Cleveland-based firm of Hewitt and Tuttle, commission merchants and produce shippers; there he learned bookkeeping. He next kept books for a prominent Cleveland miller, Arthur Quinn, at Forest City Mills and, after that, at the forwarding-and-commission house (the broker between the farmers and the market) of Hughes and Lester (founded by John and Arthur Hughes and Samuel Lester). After both John Hughes and Samuel Lester left the firm in 1862, Arthur Hughes and William established Hughes and Rockefeller, a produce-commission firm that soon became so profitable that William began to seek outside investments.

In the meantime, John D. had been achieving great success in the grain business. In 1862 he also began to invest in oil refining,

with Samuel Andrews and the brothers Maurice, Richard, and
James Clark, to form Andrews, Clark and Company. By 1865,
after separating from the Clarks and forming Rockefeller,
Andrews and Company, he convinced his brother to join the
business; the result was another new firm, William Rockefeller
and Company. The next year, William moved to New York City
to handle the company's sales-and-export business and establish
a foothold for Rockefeller and Company there. In 1867 the two
brothers and Andrews joined forces with Henry M. Flagler
and Stephen V. Harkness, combining three companies—two
in Cleveland and one in New York—as Rockefeller, Andrews
and Flagler.[10]

On January 10, 1870, with a large investment from six partners, Standard Oil was born, with John D. as president, William
as vice-president, and Flagler as secretary. The first Standard Oil
Trust was established in 1879 and the second in January 1882,
followed that August by the founding of Standard Oil of New York,
with William as president. John D. became president of Standard
Oil of Ohio, and Flagler headed Standard Oil of New Jersey.[11]

William proved to be a born merchant, and although he
often took a back seat to his more famous brother and maintained a much lower public profile, he remained throughout his
life a vital force at Standard Oil. He was modest, a man of few
words, and was always regarded by his employees and others as
scrupulously courteous. He eventually became a director of more
than forty corporations.

On May 25, 1864, William married twenty-year-old Almira
("Mira") Geraldine Goodsell, daughter of David Judson Goodsell
(whose ancestors were from Greenfield Hill, Connecticut) and
Ellen O'Brien of West Farms (in the present-day Bronx), New
York. A plainspoken woman, who thought of herself as something
of a homebody, Mira eventually settled into a lavish lifestyle
befitting the wealth that William was rapidly accumulating. The
couple established their first household in Cleveland, and in 1865
their first son, Louis Edward, was born. The boy died the following
year, a tragic loss that followed several deaths of members of

Almira Goodsell Rockefeller, about 1879 (Courtesy of the Rockefeller Archive Center)

William Rockefeller, about 1879 (Courtesy of the Rockefeller Archive Center)

Mira's family in Ohio, including that of her mother eleven years earlier at only forty-five years of age. So in 1866, when William decided to set up a base of operations for the newly formed William Rockefeller and Company in New York City, Mira was undoubtedly content to move on and start a new life.

At the same time, the large sums William was earning led him, like his brother, to seek additional and diverse investments, and to focus his energies in New York, the hub of American commerce. He began to amass large holdings in America's leading railroads, industrial companies, banks, and other enterprises— and even in some highly speculative finance ventures.[12]

Upon their arrival from Cleveland, William and Mira set up housekeeping in Fairfield, Connecticut, an easy commute from William's Manhattan office, but within a few years they decided to move their primary residence to a house on West Forty-seventh Street in New York. The family also wanted a country retreat, so William began to buy up parcels of land in Greenwich, Connecticut, in 1877 and to embark on the building of a new home that they named One Elm.[13]

Ethel Geraldine Rockefeller (she went by her first name until her late-teenage years) was the youngest of William and Mira's six children. Unfortunately, she never knew two of her brothers: Louis Edward had been just a year old when he died; and John Davison II was five at his death in 1877. Remaining were her older sister, Emma (b. 1868), and two brothers, William Goodsell (b. 1870) and Percy Avery (b. 1878). Ethel was born just three months after the second Standard Oil Trust was established and four months before William founded Standard Oil of New York. She came into a world of wealth and was able to enjoy the privileges of private school, horseback riding, servants, and a perpetual round of fine dining, theater, and travel.[14]

At the time of her birth, New York City had been growing steadily, and at times frenetically, for more than half a century. The completion in 1825 of the Erie Canal, connecting Buffalo on Lake Erie with Troy on the Hudson River, had established New York as a center of commerce and led to huge population increases.

By 1842, clean drinking water was available, piped into the Croton
Reservoir, then located at Fifth Avenue and Forty-second Street
(where the New York Public Library stands today). Cornelius
Vanderbilt's New York Central Railroad Company had dramatically
increased the number of routes into and out of the city, and when
the Atlantic telegraph cable went into service in 1866, New York
and London were directly linked for the first time. By 1870,
gaslight was available as far north as Fifty-ninth Street, adding to
the benefits of a municipal sewer system, indoor plumbing, and
central heating that many New Yorkers were already enjoying.
And in 1876, an 840-acre "labyrinth of cunningly composed
vistas and scenes," designed by the landscape architect Frederick
Law Olmsted and called Central Park, was completed.[15]

That also was the year that William and Mira built the townhouse at 689 Fifth Avenue (at the northeast corner of Fifth Avenue
and Fifty-fourth Street) in which Ethel was born. The city had
been expanding steadily northward for several decades, and
homes such as the Rockefellers' had been sprouting up throughout the area, particularly on Fifth Avenue, which was becoming
one of the finest streets not only in New York but also in the
nation. In addition to residences, beautiful churches, hotels,
and other notable buildings soon lined the avenue. St. Patrick's
Cathedral, occupying the block on Fifth Avenue from Fiftieth to
Fifty-first streets, was nearing completion, having been under
construction since 1858. The Plaza Hotel, located just north at
Fifty-ninth Street and Fifth Avenue, opened for business in 1890.
And in 1900, the University Club, designed by McKim, Mead and
White, one of the country's preeminent architectural firms, was
built on the west side of Fifth Avenue and Fifty-fourth Street. In
1913 the fourth New York building to house the Episcopal parish
of St. Thomas Church was constructed at Fifth Avenue and Fifty-
third Street, just one block south of the Rockefeller house; the
William Rockefeller family attended services there frequently.[16]

In 1886 the Rockefellers decided to move their country
residence from Greenwich, Connecticut, to the town of Mount
Pleasant, in Westchester County, New York, where the beautiful

landscape of rolling hills had already attracted wealthy landowners. About seven years later, the area would also be favored by John D., Sr., and his family, who in 1884 had moved from Cleveland to New York City. They built an estate on their sixteen-hundred-acre holdings at nearby Pocantico Hills, which they called Kykuit (Dutch for "lookout"). The proximity of the new country dwelling enabled young Ethel to socialize with her cousins, particularly John D., Jr., with whom she would maintain a lifelong friendship.[17]

Adjoining the William Rockefeller property on the south was that of Arthur Curtiss James, the son of Daniel Willis James, head of Phelps, Dodge and Company and, coincidentally, the owner of the estate in Madison, New Jersey, that Geraldine and Marcellus Hartley Dodge would purchase in 1916. On its western side, the Rockefeller property overlooked the Tappan Zee, fronting on the Hudson River for three-quarters of a mile, with an elevation of 150 feet that afforded magnificent views. To the east sprawled the picturesque hills and valleys of Westchester County. Tarrytown was three miles distant and Scarborough a mile and a half away; both were stops on the New York Central Railroad. New York City's Grand Central Station was only twenty-four miles to the south, or about forty minutes by fast train. The Tarrytown-Nyack Ferry provided frequent service westward across the Hudson.[18]

William Rockefeller bought the magnificent, approximately two-hundred-acre estate, known as Rockwood, from the heirs of William Henry Aspinwall, a New York City resident with interests in banking, shipping, and railroads as well as in civic affairs and the arts. Aspinwall had purchased the property in 1860 from his business partner, Edwin Bartlett, who in 1848 had engaged the services of the noted English architect Gervase Wheeler to build a house in the English Gothic style, 140 feet long and distinguished by a tower 80 feet high and 28 feet square. The house was filled with perpendicular tracery, frescoes, and medieval-style windows.

But the Rockefellers had an even grander property and home in mind. They began purchasing adjoining property, eventually

Pen-and-ink sketch of Rockwood Hall, the William Rockefeller country seat at Mount Pleasant, New York (Mielatz, 1911) (Courtesy of the Rockefeller Archive Center)

accumulating about eight hundred additional acres. Bartlett's house, referred to as Bartlett's Castle, was demolished to build Rockwood Hall, a castellated Elizabethan Revival mansion, with stables, that incorporated salvaged stones from Bartlett's original structure. Grounded on bedrock and built to endure for centuries, Rockwood Hall measured 174 feet long by 104 feet wide. Essentially, it was a house within a house, with a fieldstone outer wall, a four-inch air space, a brick wall, and interior walls three-and-one-half feet thick at the foundation and two feet thick on the second and third floors. Completed by the turn of the twentieth century, the main house contained some two-hundred rooms, expertly crafted by workmen brought in from Scotland and the European continent. It boasted luxuriously furnished public spaces, fourteen master bedrooms with private baths, and more than fifteen servants' bedrooms. Throughout its existence, the house would be widely known as one of the finest homes in America, second only in size and magnificence to Biltmore, the Asheville, North Carolina, estate completed in 1895 by George

The library at Rockwood Hall (Courtesy of the Rockefeller Archive Center)

Washington Vanderbilt, then and still today the largest home in America.[19]

Requiring a staff of more than sixty, Rockwood Hall featured the latest in technology and design. For example, its 400-ton-capacity stone ice house had rooms for storing meats and vegetables and boasted an ingenious refrigeration system that utilized rock salt, operating in a manner similar to an ice-cream freezer. The riding hall adjoining the stables was large enough to accommodate a three-ring circus, and the stables and stable hands' quarters covered more than three acres. Herds of cattle and Southdown sheep grazed on the rolling hills of the magnificent estate, which also included rare trees and a wildlife sanctuary for exotic game birds from Asia, Europe, and South America. Hundreds of drives, bridle paths, walks, and Italian gardens graced the extensive parklands.[20]

At Rockwood Hall the seeds were sown for Ethel's later development and accomplishments. Encouraged by her family, she spent long days riding. Even late in life, she enjoyed reminiscing about the method her brothers used to teach her to balance on a horse: they simply tied her hands behind her back! At the same time, her father instilled in her a lifelong affection for dogs, giving her an English terrier to tend when she was only six years old. The young girl caring for her first dog would, in adulthood, own, show, judge, and sell dogs; write books about them; and, ultimately, become the grand dame of the Morris and Essex Kennel Club Dog Show, the largest annual event of its kind in the world. In addition, both her parents were inveterate collectors, and Ethel came to develop an appreciation for the fine art and artifacts that they were rapidly accumulating. Antiques from all over the world, including tapestries; paintings by French, Dutch, and American masters; prints; furniture; carpets; brocade and velvet upholstery; bronzes; cloisonné; mosaics; silver; porcelains; pottery; clocks; and Chinese, Japanese, and European porcelains all were to be found at Rockwood Hall. All told, the collection was so vast that after the deaths of William and Mira, New York's Anderson Gallery had to schedule auctions over six days to dispose of it.[21]

The Rockefellers were avid buyers indeed, attending auctions and, in a few notable cases, using representatives to acquire major works of art for them. For example, in March 1887, while Rockwood Hall was under construction, William engaged the prominent collector and dealer Thomas B. Clarke to represent him at the auction of the important Alexander T. Stewart collection at Chickering Hall in New York, a sale that continued for eight straight days. Clarke bid successfully for paintings that included *The Disputed Boundary* (1869) by the British artist Erskine Nicol (1825–1904) and *The Golden Hour* (1875), a fine example of American Hudson River School painting by William Hart (1823–1894)—sophisticated choices that undoubtedly were intended for the walls of their new country seat. [22]

Mira also was an efficient and strict manager of the vast

Ethel Geraldine Rockefeller, 1891 (Courtesy of the Rockefeller Archive Center)

home and its contents. She taught her daughter well, for Ethel, later the owner and manager of Giralda Farms, would truly follow in her footsteps.

During Ethel's adolescence, the family generally stayed at Rockwood Hall on weekends and holidays, since during the week her schooling and social activities took place in New York City. She attended Miss Spence's, founded in 1892 by a young teacher, Clara Bebbe Spence, with the financial backing of Colonel and Mrs. Elliott Fitch Shephard, the parents of two of her students.

48th Street and Fifth Avenue, New York, 1899. Miss Spence's School was then located
at 6 West 48th Street, just off Fifth Avenue. (Courtesy of The Spence School)

It had been just eight years since Samuel A. Brearley had founded New York's Brearley School, a progressive institution offering
young women a program of academic subjects. Like Brearley,
Clara Spence wanted her students to receive an education
comparable to that offered the young men of the day.[23]

The school's first location was in a brownstone at 6 West
Forty-eighth Street, just off Fifth Avenue and only six blocks
from Ethel's home. Although it was often referred to as "Miss
Spence's Finishing School," it provided from the outset an education that was a far cry from the sort typically afforded wealthy
young women of the period, which was generally limited to
home management and to imparting the rituals these pupils
would need to perform as society matrons. By contrast, Spence
was progressive in its offering of thirty-nine subjects, including
American history, literature, Greek and Roman mythology, English,
French, botany, chemistry, psychology, art history, and a full

athletic program. Ethel was exposed to a curriculum not found in many private schools even today—a course of study that helped nurture her lifelong interests in history, languages, and art collecting. At the same time, Clara Spence took pains to provide Saturday-morning instruction in sewing, embroidery, and mending by having the girls make camisoles and various articles of clothing. She also made sure that her charges understood practical mathematics, in order to prepare them for household accounting. Mary Dillon Edmondson, in her book *Profiles of Leadership: A History of the Spence School*, notes that during this period, "many a father declared that he sent his daughter to Miss Spence's School because she would learn essentials of home management as well as receive an excellent education." And it was during her years at Spence that Ethel met young women who would remain her lifelong friends, two of whom were to become her neighbors after she married and moved to New Jersey, Louise Scribner and Adaline Havemeyer.[24]

In the mid-1890s, Ethel began accompanying her family on excursions to Europe. Among the first of these was an 1895 visit to Paris, during which Mira wrote to her newly engaged eldest daughter, Emma, about the family's health (particularly William's bouts with colds and "rheumatic trouble"), shopping trips, dressmakers, and the problem of finding a good photographer to take pictures of Ethel. "I feel quite discouraged," she complained. One photographer had sent eleven proofs, but Mira found them all "dreadful." This difficulty may have stemmed from the fact that Ethel was then entering the awkward period of adolescence. Only a few years later, however, she would emerge as an attractive young woman, well educated in the arts and in music and ready to enter the world of New York society.[25]

Ethel began to fill her diary with enthusiastic comments about her European travels as well as about her increasing exposure to musical performances and plays. On January 9, 1899, for example, she and Mira attended Richard Wagner's *Lohengrin* at New York's Metropolitan Opera, a performance of that popular work blessed with a perfect cast for the period, including three

Ethel Geraldine Rockefeller, about 1895
(Courtesy of St. Hubert's Giralda)

leading singers not previously heard that season. The next day, a *New York Times* reviewer noted that "there are nights and nights at the opera . . . last night was one of the happy nights." The world-renowned Jean de Reszki sang the title role; Lillian Nordica was Elsa, and Ernestine Schumann-Heink made her Metropolitan Opera debut as Ortrud. It is no wonder that Ethel pronounced it "superb" in her diary. (Indeed, she was moved to attend at least two more performances of the same opera the next year.) Later in January, a staging of Charles-François Gounod's *Romeo and Juliette*, once again with Jean de Reszki singing the title role, received the accolade, "Oh, It was so fine."[26]

Eighteen ninety-nine also was the year that the families of William and John D. Rockefeller together embarked on a ten-thousand-mile trip to Alaska. "On the *Magenta*, we begin our western trip with Uncle John's family," Gerrie—as Ethel chose to be called by this time—noted on May 27. Junior had arranged all the details, including regular Baptist services, and the Rockefellers spent five weeks traveling by boat, train, and even stagecoach before reaching their destination. Everywhere they went, Senior paused to speak to ordinary people, asking them specific questions about their concerns and reminding them to save their money. "Economy is wealth," he never tired of saying. The trip reminded him of his boyhood days, "when we went to a picnic"—despite the fact that he and his kin were now traveling in the most luxurious manner imaginable. In all, it was a most successful adventure, one that Gerrie and Junior recalled fondly for many years afterward.[27]

April 3, 1901, was her nineteenth birthday. Gerrie and her friends seem to have used the occasion to take stock of each other's characteristics. Referring to her as "Gerry-Jack," an unidentified writer noted on the inside cover of Gerrie's diary her height (5 feet, 6³/₄ inches), her coloring (tan and pink), her eyes (gray), and her hair (dark brown and curly). Her face was described as "fat," in addition to other comments related to her countenance, such as "Whole pleasing. No dimples. Good teeth." It was concluded that Gerrie looked "equally well at all times," with a good

Miss Spence's, Class of 1901. Ethel Geraldine is in the second row, third from the left. (Courtesy of The Spence School)

carriage and "excellent" figure—her attire generally reasonable and "tidy" but slated to "improve" when, in the near future, she would be able to buy her own clothes. Of most importance, especially in light of the trials and tragedies she would endure later in her life, was the itemized (if somewhat contradictory) assessment of her character: "Not easily aroused. Contented. Unsympathetic. Persevering. Tidy. Demonstrative. Patient. Independent. Careful of people's feelings. Non-depressed. Good confidante. Determined. Religious. Not extravagant. Sensitive. Not restless. Domestic. Affectionate. Cautious. Honest. Has good principles and sticks to them."[28]

The spring of 1901 was an apt time for this mutual evaluation, since it was in May that Gerrie and her friends—Louise ("Scribbie" or "Scrib"), Adaline, and Louisine ("Lula") Peters—graduated from Spence. On May 23, despite her relief at leaving her school years behind, she appeared to acknowledge the impending end of her youth: "This is the last day I shall ever go to school. I can't realize it and I am so sorry." The next morning, after a final graduation rehearsal at the famous restaurant Sherry's, Miss Spence treated them all to an ice, and that evening Adaline Havemeyer hosted a class dinner. It was a week full of celebration, capped off by the ceremony itself on May 28.[29]

The summer that ensued was probably the most carefree of her life—a constant round of parties and pleasurable pursuits. She visited The Gables (the Charles Scribner home in Morristown, New Jersey), and then Broadlawn (the Morris Plains, New Jersey, estate of her sister, Emma, and her husband, Dr. D. Hunter McAlpin). There, Gerrie rode, dined, attended July Fourth fireworks, and danced at a cotillion arranged by the Scribners. From New Jersey, it was on to take part in family activities at Islip, Long Island, followed by a trip to the summer lodge and fifty-thousand-acre forest preserve her father had purchased in 1899 at Bay Pond, in New York's Adirondack Mountains.[30]

This cycle of activities was typical for wealthy young women of the time. Grand tours also were common, and so Gerrie began planning an extensive and elaborate trip to Europe, to begin in late March 1903. Since she was not to be accompanied by her family, the Rockefellers, like other wealthy and socially prominent families of the time, sought to provide their daughter with a suitable female companion and chaperone. They found her in Caroline Woodruff North, who came to live with them after Gerrie had made her acquaintance at various charity events. North was a young widow who had been boarding with friends in Elizabeth, New Jersey, after the death of her husband, a New Jersey shirt manufacturer. In February 1902, Gerrie noted an evening at the Boston Symphony that the two women attended, and during the following month, Mrs. North was included in a family visit to Palm Beach.[31]

On March 28, 1903, just a few days before her twenty-first birthday, Gerrie, Mrs. North, and Gerrie's cousin Mary (probably Mary Brockway) sailed on the *König Albert*, arriving in Naples on April 9. After visiting Pompeii, Sorrento, and Capri, they went on to Rome, where they stayed for two weeks. They visited not only the major tourist attractions but also places Gerrie had undoubtedly learned about in art history courses at Miss Spence's school. There was the Church of San Pietro in Vincoli, containing the supposed chains of St. Peter, where Gerrie took particular note of Michelangelo's statue of Moses. A visit to the Baptistery of Giovanni di Laterano provided a view of "fine mosaics in oratory and chapels and beautiful bronze doors." The next day found them at St. Peter's Basilica, where Gerrie was greatly taken with the "bronze statue of St. Peter whose toe is so worn with kisses." They toured the Vatican galleries and the Sistine Chapel, the temples of Vesta and Fortuna, the Church of Santa Maria in Trastevere, and numerous other sites and museums. The young women also shopped, dined, and even managed to be on hand, on April 27, for a procession of kings that included England's Edward VII and Italy's Victor Emmanuel III.[32]

After Rome, Gerrie and her party moved on to Orvieto, Perugia, Siena, and Genoa, then across the border into southern France, where they visited Monte Carlo, Nice, and Marseilles. They arrived in Paris by train on May 13 and stayed for eleven days, where shopping at Bon Marché, attending the theater and opera, and visiting museums occupied most of their time. After visiting the border city of Strasbourg, Germany was next—with stops in Frankfurt, Dresden, Berlin, and Cologne—followed by the Low Countries, where they toured The Hague, Amsterdam, Antwerp, Bruges, and Brussels. It was then back to Paris for three weeks until July 8, when they crossed the English Channel and continued on to London. There the trio was united with Louise Scribner, who was traveling with her parents. They spent a week together, shopping, dining, and touring, before the Scribners left via Paris for the United States on July 15. A week later, Gerrie and her party followed on the *Kaiser Wilhelm der Grosse.* It was a whirlwind trip—the most exciting she had known. But she also realized that she would somehow have to come down to earth, noting in her diary on July 30 that the "trip is over now and must settle down." Yet she wasn't really ready to take her own advice, because during the next few years she continued to travel extensively, broadening the education in art history she had begun at Spence and further developing the aesthetic tastes that would shape her outlook as a collector for the rest of her life.[33]

Gerrie also seemed to be on a mission of self-improvement during these years of early womanhood. She studied languages and soon was inserting lines in French as well as German in her diary—mostly ideas about love, jealousy, and friendship. She made careful note of the books she had read while abroad, a long and varied list of works popular among young women of the day, including James M. Barrie's *Sentimental Tommy* and *The Little White Bird*, as well as more serious volumes, such as Henryk Sienkiewicz's *Quo Vadis* and Émile Zola's *Rome*.[34]

Although Gerrie had already traveled extensively, had attended her first prom at age eighteen, and had begun to ride at the Westchester Horse Show when she was twenty, it was not until 1903, at twenty-one, that she made a serious entrance into the world of society—regularly attending cotillions, "cake walks," and other such events.

Yet traveling, particularly in Europe, remained her deepest interest. In May 1904, again with Mrs. North as her companion, Gerrie sailed to Plymouth on the *Deutschland*. They went directly to Paris, where they deepened their acquaintance with significant collections and cultural monuments, including Sainte-Chapelle, the Pantheon, and Nôtre Dame. They dined regularly at the famed Tour d'Argent and spent evenings at the theater, the Opéra Comique, and the Moulin Rouge. On June 5, they recrossed the English Channel, enjoyed the museums and theaters of London, motored throughout Scotland, returned to England, and in the third week of July sailed back home aboard the *Arabic*. Gerrie spent the rest of the summer commuting between her parents' Bay Pond Home in the Adirondacks and friends' homes in New Jersey, where she was entertained in Morristown by the Scribners and their neighbors, the Van Beurens, and also in Morris Plains by her sister, Emma, and brother-in-law, Hunter. In December she visited Quebec but returned to New York in time to hear a performance of Handel's *Messiah* at St. Thomas Church just before Christmas.[35]

On February 7, 1905, Gerrie and Mrs. North sailed for France on the *Kaiser Wilhelm der Grosse* for an extended European tour with an itinerary that had them arriving in a new city almost daily. Again they dined, shopped, and toured, meeting up with William and Mira in May for a few weeks in Paris. Gerrie stayed on with Mrs. North until November 3, when they departed Liverpool on the *Arabic* for New York.[36]

Later that month, Gerrie visited her friend Scrib, who by this time was living with her husband, George Schieffelin, at the Sycamores in Convent Station, New Jersey, a house the Scribners had purchased for Louise and their new son-in-law adjacent to their own estate. Scrib's new life appealed to Gerrie. "She has a darling baby and attractive house," she noted in her diary. But the idea of settling down would still have to wait, for Gerrie had planned yet another trip to England and France, to begin on November 29 on the *Oceanic* and to continue into June 1906. While visiting Cannes in January 1906, she sat for Friedrich August von Kaulbach (1850–1920), a German artist popular among European royalty and society. Kaulbach's two extant portraits of Gerrie reveal an attractive, confident, and mature young woman.[37]

# CHAPTER II

# MARCELLUS HARTLEY DODGE

*Love is sadness, love is madness,*
*Love's a smile and love's a sigh.*
*Love will rule you, love will fool you,*
*Love is sorrow, but tomorrow*
*Love will bring you joy again,*
*Love is truly most unruly,*
*Love is sunshine after rain.*

—Attributed to Geraldine Rockefeller Dodge[1]

The date of the first meeting of Geraldine Rockefeller and Marcellus Hartley Dodge is unknown. She first mentions him in her diary on October 6, 1906, during a visit with her sister and brother-in-law at Broadlawn, noting a "fine motor trip with Marcellus Dodge . . . to the Oranges." Three weeks later, the pair went riding and, the next day, attended church together. By November 11, she was referring to him by his nickname: "Marcy went to church with me, then came to lunch and spent the afternoon at the Bronx." Two days later, "Marcy came to dinner." On Sunday, November 18, the single entry in her diary reads "MHD."[2]

Just after the dawn of the new century, many of Gerrie's relatives and good friends were getting married. In 1901 Gerrie served as a bridesmaid at the wedding of her brother Percy to Isabel Stillman, daughter of James Stillman, one of her father's business partners. Later that year, Junior married Abby Aldrich. On April 5, 1904, Louise Scribner wed George Schieffelin of Morristown at St. Bartholomew's Church in New York City, and on October 30, 1906, Gerrie noted in her diary the engagement of Adaline Havemeyer to Peter H. B. Frelinghuysen. Just two weeks later, on November 14, another schoolmate, Louisine (Lula) Peters, was married at Grace Church in New York. Gerrie's November 18 entry may have signified her engagement to Marcellus Dodge; in any event, the formal announcement would not be made until March.[3]

Gerrie and Marcy began making wedding plans late in 1906, and by the end of January had visited Dr. Ernest M. Stires, rector of St. Thomas Church, to arrange for him to preside at their nuptials. On February 12, the pair traveled to Nyack, New York, so that Marcy could introduce Gerrie to his father and stepmother, Mr. and Mrs. Norman White Dodge. It was well that they met when they did, for Norman died suddenly just eight days later, at age sixty.[4]

Marcy was a descendant of two prominent English families. His father's ancestors arrived in Salem, Massachusetts, in 1629. By 1818, the family had relocated to New York City, where Marcy's paternal grandfather, William Earl Dodge (1805–1883), began his mercantile career and, in 1828, married Melissa Phelps, daughter of Anson G. Phelps. Five years later, Dodge entered into a partnership with his father-in-law in the metal business to form Phelps, Dodge and Company.[5]

On his mother's side, Marcy's early ancestors included one Sir Hartley, who had been knighted in 1663 by King Charles II, and a Reverend Hartley, the Vicar of Armley, in York. Isaac Hartley, Marcy's maternal great-great grandfather, arrived in America in 1797, settling at Charlton in Saratoga County, New York. His grandfather, the original Marcellus Hartley, who was born on September 23, 1828, began his career as a clerk in his father's mercantile business at age seventeen. After three years, he went to work for Francis Tomes and Sons, dealers in fine guns, hardware, and sporting goods. In 1854, at twenty-six,

Marcellus, J. Rutsen Schuyler, and Malcolm Graham became
partners to form Schuyler, Hartley and Graham, Importers and
Manufacturers of Guns, Pistols and Fancy Goods. The following
year, he married Frances Chester White, daughter of Dr. Samuel
Pomeroy White of New York City. They would have three daughters, including Marcy's mother, Emma.[6]

By the beginning of the Civil War, Schuyler, Hartley and
Graham was operating the largest sporting goods establishment
in America, but scrupulously avoiding selling arms it produced to
the South or, in fact, to any parties Hartley suspected of clandes-
tine shipments to the Confederates. In the first months of 1862,
as stocks of weapons in federal and state armories became deplet-
ed and domestic manufacturers were finding it difficult to meet
the demands of the Union Army, President Lincoln grew desper-
ate for a source of weapons. He began looking for a means to
divert European arms deliveries intended for the South, which
were being routed through the British island of Nassau. With a
Northern blockade of Southern ports proving less than effective,
Lincoln and his Secretary of War, Edwin M. Stanton, reached out
for advice to New York's Governor Edwin D. Morgan. The governor enthusiastically suggested that they send Marcellus Hartley
to Nassau to buy arms. Hartley quickly left for Washington to
discuss the matter with Lincoln, but by the time he reached the
White House, he had come to the conclusion that the best means
to cut off shipments of arms to the South would be to go to
where they were being produced—the manufacturing centers
of Europe. He offered to travel there himself to accomplish the
mission and also to corner the arms market, an approach that
won Lincoln's immediate approval. In July 1862, Hartley, with his
wife and three daughters in tow, traveled to England and then
to Liège, the arms center of Belgium, and after that to every place
on the Continent where good guns were to be found. He sought
out the appropriate manufacturers and promised immediate payment for their stocks in order to force cancellation of Southern
contracts. Then, using astute negotiating skills, Hartley kept
prices within reason. And, in order to help assure delivery to

Northern ports, he even arranged for chartered steamers. Most important, by the time he returned to America in April 1863, he had successfully diverted Europe's arms output, a feat that proved to be of enormous help to the Union cause.[7]

After the war, Hartley decided to expand his business interests by manufacturing bullets, establishing the Union Metallic Cartridge Company in Bridgeport, Connecticut. By 1888, he also had acquired the Remington Arms Company, based in Ilion, New York. He proved to be an extremely successful industrialist and entrepreneur, eventually accumulating a fortune of more than $50 million.

Emma Hartley and Norman Dodge were married on May 6, 1880. Born on February 28, 1881, Marcy was their first and only child: Emma died only two days later at the age of 22. Despite this early tragedy, Marcy spent a pleasant and comfortable childhood in the New York home of his maternal grandparents at 232 Madison Avenue, reared primarily by his grandmother and his aunt Helen Hartley Jenkins after his widowed father left him in their care. Educated at the John A. Browning School in New York, Marcy went on to Columbia University, where he headed the campus branch of the Young Men's Christian Association, served as manager of the track team and coxswain of the rowing crew, and joined the Psi Upsilon fraternity.

In January 1902, during Marcy's junior year in college, his grandfather Marcellus died suddenly while attending a business meeting. Although a large part of his estate was left to his widow and to his surviving daughter, Marcy was his major heir. It was an enormous inheritance and, at the same time, a burden the young man had not expected to assume for many years. But Marcy enjoyed the confidence and support of both his grandmother and his aunt, and so with their encouragement and approval, he became the president and board chairman of Remington Arms; vice-president of the Union Metallic Cartridge Company (which later consolidated with Remington); president of the Bridgeport Gun Implement Company; a director of the Equitable Life Assurance Society, the International Banking

Company and M. Hartley Company; and a board member of the Delaware, Lackawanna and Western Railroad. In addition, he oversaw the family's continued support of Hartley House, a settlement house founded by his maternal great-grandfather, the early-nineteenth-century philanthropist Robert Milham Hartley, at 413 West Forty-sixth Street in New York, and of Hartley House Farm, a "resort" for New York's poor children established on the family's New Jersey property.[8]

Marcy, still a full-time student at Columbia, was clearly young and inexperienced. But he readily grasped how hard he would have to work to assume his multiple new management roles. Moreover, he had the good sense to realize that inheriting an enormous amount of money was a responsibility not to be taken lightly. He spent every Saturday at his late grandfather's desk, poring over documents and background information. The burdens were there, but so was the incredible good fortune that inspired his classmates at Columbia to vote him the "luckiest" member of the class of 1903. By 1912, Marcy's continuing diligence so impressed his grandmother that she turned over her remaining stock in the companies to him. His subsequent offer to purchase his aunt's stock also was graciously accepted, since she wanted the businesses to remain within the family.[9]

In 1905, when Marcy was just twenty-four, Adolph Ochs, owner of *The New York Times*, appealed to him for a loan to pay off a debt to the Dodge-family-owned Equitable Life Assurance Society, and to borrow an additional $300,000, in exchange for which he would pledge his fifty-one percent of *Times* stock as collateral. (There was a precedent for this request: Marcellus Hartley had extended a loan to Ochs in 1896, after the *Times* was thrown into receivership as a result of a major drop in its circulation due to the success of several sensation-mongering New York papers of the period.) Marcy was sympathetic to Ochs's request and prepared to provide the funds, but he also realized that the *Times* had given editorial support to a public investigation of insurance scandals that was then under way—so he insisted that the transaction remain confidential. Ochs assured him that it would, and

he kept his word; he repaid the loan in 1916. Thus Marcellus
Hartley and then Marcellus Hartley Dodge had rescued the
newspaper twice in its history.[10]

It also fell to Marcy to maintain ties, as had his grandfather
before him, with his alma mater, Columbia University. In 1903 he
and his aunt Helen Hartley Jenkins (who would serve as a trustee
of Columbia University's Teachers College from 1907 to 1935)
gave the school $300,000 to build Hartley Hall, an undergraduate
dormitory completed in 1905; in later years, he contributed
$50,000 to help renovate the facility. He went on to establish
scholarships and to provide funding for other campus buildings,
including Ferris Booth Hall, the university's student center
completed in 1956; the old business school building, which was
renamed Dodge Hall in 1965; and the physical fitness building
constructed in 1974. In 1907 Marcy became the youngest man
ever elected to Columbia's board of trustees. He served as its
clerk from 1923 until his retirement from the board in 1959,
the year he was elected trustee emeritus. While on the board, he
participated in graduations and many ceremonies at the school,
including visits by Queen Marie of Rumania in October 1926
and by Great Britain's King George and Queen Elizabeth in
June 1939.[11]


### EARLY MARRIED LIFE

Marcy and Gerrie announced their engagement on March 19,
1907—Mira Rockefeller's birthday—during a family dinner. Only
a month later, on April 18, the couple wed at the Rockefellers'
New York City townhouse. The William and John D. Rockefeller
families joined the Hartleys, Jenkinses, and Dodges in witnessing
the marriage. As planned, Dr. Stires presided at the 4 p.m. ceremony, which was kept low key in deference to the groom, who
was still mourning the passing of his father barely two months
earlier. Nevertheless, Mira had the rooms decorated appropriately
with beautiful silk ribbons as well as with bridesmaid's roses and

Marcellus Hartley Dodge, 1907 (Courtesy of St. Hubert's Giralda)

Wedding photograph of Geraldine Rockefeller Dodge, 1907 (Courtesy of St. Hubert's Giralda)

palms brought from Rockwood Hall. Gerrie wore no jewelry, also in deference to the death of Marcy's father, but she was gowned in magnificent white satin with tulle and lace, and a tulle veil. She carried white flowers.[12]

With Marcy's enormous inheritance and Gerrie's family wealth, it is no wonder that at the time of their marriage, they were hailed as the richest young couple in America. Indeed, the wealth and prominence of the family of Marcellus Hartley Dodge certainly rivaled that of the Rockefellers, and the hardworking nature of Marcy's forebears matched the industriousness of both William and John D. Rockefeller.

For Gerrie, the months that followed the wedding were filled with optimism and happiness—"blissful days," she called them. The newlyweds had taken only a brief honeymoon at a location identified by Gerrie in her diary as "Daffodil Farm" (in Valhalla, New York); they preferred to wait until summer to go on a more

Geraldine Rockefeller Dodge at Versailles on her
honeymoon, 1907 (Courtesy of the Rockefeller
Archive Center)

extended trip, to Europe. Marcy had to travel on business during
June, and Gerrie found herself eagerly awaiting his return. Her
typically succinct diary entries could not disguise her content-
ment, for on June 23 she noted, "Marcy returned only this morning, I'm so happy again." On July 4, "M and I spent quiet but
beautiful day together."[13]

On August 14, the couple departed on the *Adriatic*, headed
for France and England. They toured Paris, Fontainebleau, and
Versailles, and traveled to Caen in northern France. In London
they saw the famous Wallace Collection and enjoyed the theater.
They returned to New York on September 13.[14]

Gerrie and Marcy decided to establish a country residence in
Morris County, New Jersey. Marcy's grandmother and aunt lived
in the Morristown area, and Gerrie's sister, Emma, and her husband maintained a large estate, Broadlawn, in nearby Morris
Plains. At first, they rented a home in Convent Station (the
Schmidt house), opposite the Morris County Golf Club entrance
at Madison Avenue and Canfield Way. But soon they moved to
Honeymoon Cottage, also known as Two Shoes, a lovely, ram-
bling, old-fashioned seventeen-room house set behind a large
stone wall on Hartley's family estate on Spring Valley Road in
Harding Township, New Jersey. They also built a separate field-
stone house containing a playroom for their first and only child,
Marcellus Hartley Dodge, Jr., who was born on July 29, 1908, at
Rockwood Hall. In addition, a few years after their marriage,
William and Mira decided to build a house for the young couple
at 691 Fifth Avenue, next door and connected to their own
home—a practice that was then quite common among wealthy
New York families.[15]

The Dodges led a tranquil life until the outbreak of World
War I in Europe in August 1914. The unprecedented scale of the
conflict led France and England to seek quick and substantial
increases in their stocks of available arms. Although Remington
had traditionally devoted itself to selling firearms to American
sportsmen, the Allies turned to the company to fill their needs,
offering it enormous contracts that far exceeded the capacity of

its factories. Marcy, as chairman of Remington's board of directors, and Samuel F. Pryor, the company's president, realized that to fill potentially huge orders, it would have to expand its production capacity vastly—an undertaking requiring many millions of dollars. Marcy agreed to make this risky investment in expansion, because it was clear that if the Allies lacked sufficient up-to-date weapons, their defeat would be inevitable. Remington began to meet the need by producing Lebel rifles for France, then accepted an order from England for a million Enfield rifles, with a potential request for the manufacture of another million. But when these initial orders came in, the company's production capacity limited it to fewer than five hundred guns a day. To meet the contract deadlines, Marcy realized that he would have to raise that figure to two thousand per day. He did this with a lavish expenditure of money as well as with tremendous cooperation on the part of Remington Arms officials, engineers, and workers. It was an accomplishment that was regarded as an industrial miracle.[16]

Having met these extraordinary production demands, Remington was widely perceived as able to succeed at almost any small-arms-and-ammunition manufacturing challenge. In 1915, spurred by an order from the Imperial Russian Government for a million rifles and a hundred million rounds of ammunition, Marcy borrowed more than $40 million to build additional production facilities. There didn't seem to be any choice.

Even though Americans were not yet fighting in the war, it was having a dramatic impact on them. Writing in her diary on May 8, 1915, Gerrie responded to the sinking of the *Lusitania* just the day before by noting "everybody horror struck with the Lusitania catastrophe." Like all Americans, Marcy and Gerrie had been outraged to hear and read of the disaster, in which 128 civilian passengers had died. Eight years earlier, they had returned from their honeymoon on the same ship, and as recently as the summer of 1914, they also had traveled to England and back on the *Lusitania*—returning one month after the outbreak of the war.[17]

The sinking of the *Lusitania* seemed to make Marcy's decision to create additional Remington plants, primarily in Bridgeport, Connecticut, all the more justified. Yet filling the Russian order was going to be difficult. Besides the vast sums of money needed to gear up for production, Remington workers would constantly be watched by a contingent of up to fifteen–hundred inspectors. These included Cossacks, wearing full Russian army regalia, whom the Russian government sent to provide continuing first-hand assurance that it was not being cheated. The atmosphere was made even more tense by reports that enemy saboteurs were hatching plans to undermine production. Indeed, there were some attempts to cause explosions and wreck machinery, but the hiring of additional guards and the security of a U.S. destroyer patrolling the Bridgeport harbor successfully diffused the threat. No serious cases of sabotage occurred in any of Remington's factories.

The biggest problem, however, involved finances. Marcy had to find lenders willing to extend credit until the Russian rifles came into full production; he was able to do so with the assistance of William Rockefeller's lawyers. With Rockefeller's backing, the necessary extension of time was secured. By February 1917, things were looking up: the millions of dollars invested in the new plants were yielding the high level of production hoped for to meet the Russians' requirements. But on March 16, just when success finally seemed to be assured, Czar Nicholas II abdicated, the government fell, and all contracts into which it had entered were repudiated.[18]

For Remington Arms, the cancellation of the Russian contract was a disaster; it would be impossible to repay the huge loans. The labor force, mainly in Bridgeport, was thrown out of work, and hundreds of thousands of new rifles sat in warehouses. Marcy worried not only about his own financial loss but also about his employees. "Each night when I tried to go to sleep," he lamented, "I lay there thinking that I had nothing left of all I had once owned, and that I had no further employment for the thousands of men who had worked hard and loyally during the days of stress."[19]

But this dire situation would soon change. The 1915 sinking of the *Lusitania*, the continuing ruthlessness of German U-boats, and finally Germany's announcement in January 1917 that it would conduct unlimited submarine warfare combined to lead President Woodrow Wilson to sever diplomatic relations between the two countries. On April 2, 1917, despite the fact that the United States was not militarily prepared, Wilson asked Congress for a declaration of war; it was issued four days later. Before 1917, Wilson had been convinced that domestic production of armaments compromised the position of neutrality he believed it was necessary for the nation to maintain. But now that war was declared, the United States needed weapons enough to equip four million troops within a matter of months. To satisfy this demand, the government would have to give financial assistance to the nation's arms manufacturers so that they could adequately gear up for production. For Remington, this assistance came in the form of an outright purchase of 600,000 of the 750,000 rifles already manufactured for Russia, thereby substantially reducing Marcy's loss and saving the company from ruin.[20]


GIRALDA FARMS

Before the onset of Marcy's financial problems of 1916, the Dodges had decided to move to Madison, New Jersey. Originally called Bottle Hill (allegedly after a local tavern), the community was founded in 1740 by James and David Burnet. In 1834 it was renamed Madison, in honor of James Madison, fourth president of the United States. Three years later the railroad arrived, creating a suburban enclave popular with commuters who worked in Newark and New York. By the late 1850s, the community became home to scores of rose growers and greenhouses, whose enterprises were so successful that Madison came to be known as "The Rose City," a title it retains to this day. In 1866 the Methodist Theological School was founded at Drew University. On Christmas Eve, 1889, Madison Borough was formally incorporated.[21]

The Dodges decided to purchase Onunda, an Elizabethan Revival mansion, situated on some 240 acres, that had been built and named in 1893 by Daniel Willis James, president of the Curtiss Securities Company, and a vice-president of Phelps, Dodge and Company. In his day, he was Madison's largest benefactor, having provided funding for such projects as James Park, which opened in July 1898, and, in 1899, having completely underwritten construction of the borough's first library—a magnificent Romanesque Revival structure designed by the Boston firm of Charles Brigham and Willard P. Adden and clearly modeled on Henry Hobson Richardson's famous Trinity Church in Boston (1877). James was obviously an admirer of Richardson, who had died thirteen years earlier. The library opened on May 30, 1900, with a collection of five-thousand volumes.[22]

After James died in 1907, his widow, Ellen Stebbins James, stayed on at Onunda until her death in May 1916. Keenly aware of his parents' devotion to the property, Arthur Curtiss James, executor of the estate, found it difficult to sell, mournfully remarking to a local reporter that "it will be a hard wrench for me to give it up." Yet sell it he did, that July, to the Dodges.

For Gerrie and Marcy, Onunda was rich with possibilities. Thinking of his own interests and as well as those of Marcy, William Rockefeller saw it as a fine place to raise horses. Gerrie appeared to have other plans, for she had already become interested in the breeding of purebred dogs. She changed the estate's name to Giralda, a reference to St. Geraldo, the Spanish patron of orphans, and began adapting the thirty-five-room mansion to suit her family's needs. For example, she added roofed porches, which as Marcy's cousin Helen Hartley Mead Platt recalled, cut down on the light that entered the house. Yet Helen also remembered the place as having a certain degree of charm. An unused bowling alley became home to a train collection given to young Hartley, as Gerrie and Marcy's son became known. A pipe organ was installed (Gerrie had taken lessons on this instrument), and a swimming pool was built on the grounds. Gerrie also began

acquiring rare species of plants, shrubs, and trees—from dwarf
Japanese maples to beautiful flowering varieties.[23]

Over the years, the landholdings of the estate grew, eventually
including the adjoining properties of L. L. Dunham (formerly the
Charles Harkness estate), F. Hallett Lovell, and others. Eventually,
it encompassed more than 370 acres, primarily in Madison. At
the same time, Marcy retained the Hartley Farms estate, including
Hartley House on Spring Valley Road, which he had inherited
and planned to give to young Hartley when he grew up. It provided additional office and entertaining space. An eighty-foot-wide-
trail was created to link the two residences.[24]

Maintaining this vast acreage and its numerous structures
required forty to fifty workers, in addition to the large house
staffs. Several employees lived in houses that the Dodges provided—generally on streets adjoining the estate. According to
Mary Jane Ellis, who was Gerrie's trusted friend and companion
in later years, she was a considerate employer who felt a great
sense of responsibility toward those who were loyal to her and
to her family.[25]

As the Dodges continued to build their lives in New Jersey,
William and Mira Rockefeller aged and became increasingly
infirm. Gerrie and Marcy visited them often at 689 Fifth Avenue,
at Rockwood Hall, and at Indian Mound, the Rockefeller winter
home on Jekyll Island, off the coast of Georgia. William was
regularly plagued with indigestion, neuralgia, and various throat
ailments. And, by 1919, Mira had developed serious heart problems—a "heart slump" she called it—causing her to be bedridden
for longer and longer periods. Although Mira did not dwell on
these infirmities in her letters, William wrote Gerrie about them.
In early 1919, for example, he noted that she had been in bed for
several days, "a little rundown, quite nervous."[26]

Next pages: The main house at Giralda Farms
(Courtesy of the *Madison Eagle* and the Madison
Public Library)

The onset of Mira's illness and the increasing confinement it brought appear to have elicited interests that had taken a back seat to more domestic concerns in her earlier years. By 1917, Mira had begun reading about and commenting on issues related to politics and even foreign policy, and she repeatedly requested books on the subjects. As America entered the war with Germany, she wrote Gerrie that she hoped "our country will not let sentiment run away with their judgment." Later, she compared the enemy, "the Huns," with the German Hessians whom the British had hired to help them fight during the American Revolution. She could "remember hearing my father tell about the sacking of Fairfield [Connecticut]," when the Hessians had "pillaged houses" and the women and children had been "sent back in the country." (Mira's great-grandfather Louis Goodsell had fought in the Revolutionary War.) While confined to bed in March 1919, she expressed her concerns about commitments Woodrow Wilson appeared to be making at the Versailles Peace Conference. "Will a patriot arise and lead us out of the trap into which we have fallen?" she wondered. Yet it seems that her interest in domestic details also remained strong, as she discussed gifts to Gerrie of carpets and other decorative items for Giralda. She appeared to enjoy her daughter's ever-growing interest in art, while maintaining firm opinions concerning the quality of artists and sculptors. Just three days before her death, she wrote Gerrie that [Rosa] Bonheur is "in my estimation far ahead of many [Sir Edwin] Landseers."[27]

Mira died at Indian Mound in January 1920; she was seventy-seven. For over a week prior to her death, William had filled his diary with notes on the progress of her recovery from "neuralgia." And although she had seemed to be gaining, he reported, during the night of January 17 "without any warning [she] suddenly died while sitting in her chair." "All days alike. Sad and awful," Gerrie noted in her diary two days after her mother's burial on January 21 at Sleepy Hollow Cemetery in Sleepy Hollow, New York. She had been the heart of the William Rockefeller family, and although she was sometimes thought of as strict and unyielding, she was nonetheless deeply mourned by her four children.[28]

William Rockefeller visiting his old home in Moravia, New York, 1922
(Courtesy of O. Stillman Rockefeller)

William carried on as normally as possible, spending winters
on Jekyll Island and summers at Bay Pond in the Adirondacks,
with spring and autumn divided between 689 Fifth Avenue and
Rockwood Hall. By early 1922, the lonely widower found himself
befriended on Jekyll Island by a woman much younger than himself (probably Marion Bourne), identified only as "Sweetie" by
Gerrie's worried brother William G.; he felt their father was both
flattered by the woman's attentions and becoming too dependant
on her. But this state of affairs was not to last. In June 1922, the
elder William, accompanied by a party including John D., John D.,
Jr., and Marcy, left on a four-day, 738-mile car trip that included a
visit to their early boyhood home, in New York state. It was the
third such trip the brothers had made since 1919; it seemed to be
becoming an annual event. As he had in the past, young Hartley
(now almost fourteen) also joined them, serving as the party's
photographer. Although fatigued on his return and prone to
catching cold, William reported to his office bright and early on
each of the next two days. But on his second day back, he got
caught in the rain. The resulting head cold progressed rapidly to
pneumonia, and on June 24, despite receiving diligent medical
care at Rockwood Hall, he passed away. Gerrie and her extended
family were once again thrown into mourning. William was

buried at Sleepy Hollow Cemetery on June 26. In December he
was reinterred, with Mira and their son William G., who had died
suddenly the previous Thanksgiving Day, in the doorless crypt
of the newly completed marble-and-granite family mausoleum
on the cemetery's highest site.[29]

Nearly eighty-two at his death, William Rockefeller was
generally considered to be one of the wealthiest men in America,
with a reported gross estate totaling more than $100 million,
largely in Standard Oil securities. His will divided his holdings
into trust funds for his four children, and the contents of
Rockwood Hall and the family's numerous collections were
ordered sold at auction by the Anderson Gallery of New York.
Gerrie and Emma then set about distributing some of their parents' personal possessions within the family. For example, pins
were made from Mira's diamonds for their brother Percy's daughters, Gladys and Faith. But Gerrie held onto other items, some of
them for decades. In a 1951 letter to her nephew William, she
commented that "at the time of the dispersal of [William and
Mira's] estate we took a lot of things we actually did not need as
a good many things had your grandmother's and grandfather's
names on them, and they were prejudiced against their getting
into strangers' possession. They used to enjoy attending the
auction sales and often came back and said, 'How pathetic it was
to see the family possessions with their names on them, etc. going
under the block.'" She noted happily that William's daughter
Elsie and son-in-law Bill were showing some appreciation for
"so-called heirlooms," adding ruefully that many young people
"scorn the possession of anything that has come down to them
or isn't of the very latest style."[30]

For Gerrie, the passing of her parents truly meant the end of
her youth. She now concentrated increasingly on her life in her
adopted state, New Jersey, and would focus her energies there for
the rest of her days.

# CHAPTER III

# MARCELLUS HARTLEY DODGE, JR.

*His eager feet were just at the threshold of adult life.*
*Youth, glorious, vivid, pulsating youth was his,*
*and how he enjoyed it.*

—From a eulogy for Marcellus Hartley Dodge, Jr.,
September 11, 1930

An only child, Hartley was clearly adored by his family. Yet according to friends, family, and the estate staff, he remained an unspoiled, well-mannered boy and young adult.

Hartley fit well into all of the Rockefeller households, and visits to his aunts, uncles, and cousins were common during his early years. When Gerrie and Marcy traveled, he often stayed with his grandparents at Rockwood Hall with his German nanny, whom the family called "Fräulein." On those occasions, Mira revealed herself to be something of a doting grandmother as she busied herself with her young grandson, concentrating on improving his reading as well as keeping him amused. In 1914, while the Dodges were in Europe, she wrote Gerrie that Hartley's "tricycle was too small so have given him a larger one for his birthday."[1]

Through his early years, Hartley exhibited a fascination for anything and everything mechanical—from the collection of trains he received as a child to a passion for aviation as he

The William Rockefeller family, about 1909
Front row: William Rockefeller McAlpin, Geraldine Rockefeller McAlpin,
Isabel Rockefeller, David Hunter McAlpin III

Middle row: Isabel Stillman Rockefeller, James Stillman Rockefeller,
Avery Rockefeller, Winifred Rockefeller, Elsie Stillman Rockefeller,
Almira Geraldine Rockefeller, Elaine Rockefeller McAlpin, Emma Rockefeller McAlpin

Back row: William Goodsell Rockefeller, Godfrey Stillman Rockefeller, David Hunter
McAlpin, Jr., William Rockefeller, Marcellus Hartley Dodge, Marcellus Hartley Dodge, Jr.,
Geraldine Rockefeller Dodge
(Courtesy of the Rockefeller Archive Center)

Gerrie and Hartley at the launching of the S.S. *Sucubaco*
at the Newark (N.J.) Bay shipyard in February 1921.
Gerrie was the sponsor of the Port Newark ship, which
she baptized with an American brand of champagne.
(Courtesy of St. Hubert's Giralda)

MORRIS ROSENFEL
N.Y.

Gerrie and Hartley, about 1922
(Courtesy of the Rockefeller Archive Center)

reached his maturity. After developing an interest in photography, he took to accompanying and taking pictures of his grandfather William and great-uncle John D. on trips, beginning in 1919 with a visit to the haunts of their childhood in upstate New York. Like his father, he enjoyed horseback riding. Gerrie's trusted stableman, Harry Thoman, taught Hartley to handle horses, and for several years, the pair was a common sight as they rode together through the woods of the Dodge estates.

Hartley's early education began at his father's alma mater, the John A. Browning School in New York City, followed by boarding school at the Loomis Institute in Windsor, Connecticut. There he was a member of the football squad and French club. He also served as stage manager for the drama club and as a staff member of the school paper. In 1926, as graduation approached, the question of which college he would attend inevitably arose; and needless to say, since his father was a noted alumnus as well as a trustee, Columbia University ranked high on his list of choices. But on the other hand, as Grace Hartley Mead, Marcy's cousin, and her daughter Helen Hartley Mead Platt recalled, "the McAlpin family boys were going to Princeton." His cousin William McAlpin (son of his Aunt Emma and Uncle Hunter) was just completing his education there. On the Rockefeller side, Junior's son John D. III was enrolled as a member of the class of 1929. It was a difficult decision, but Hartley chose to study engineering at Princeton.[2]

During the summer of 1926, before his freshman year, Hartley traveled to the Canadian Rockies with three friends, a trip that included mountain climbing under the direction of an engineer who had mapped the Rockies for the Canadian government. The following summer, he entered the fifteen-foot boat races in Edgartown, Massachusetts. And in 1928, he toured extensively in the West, beginning in Livingston, Montana, with Dick Randall, who had earlier guided Theodore Roosevelt and other prominent people on local tours from his nearby ranch. Hartley visited Yellowstone Park and attended the Livingston rodeo, where he surprised his companions by appearing in the ring riding a steer.[3]

Hartley's deepest interests, stretching back to boyhood, concerned mechanics, locomotives, and the then relatively new field of aeronautics. While at Princeton, he earned a pilot's license for private flying, a hobby that distressed his mother. But that pursuit appeared to be acceptable to Marcy, who purchased land and began constructing a flying field near the family's New Jersey property for Hartley's use. His advisor at college, Dr. Luther P. Eisenhart, the dean of Princeton's graduate school, reported that the young man's primary interest was in applied science. Like

Hartley, Eisenhart's son, Churchill, was fascinated by aeronautics, and the two visited often at the dean's Princeton home.[4]

Hartley's years at Princeton were happy and successful. Known by his friends as "Doogie" and as "Hart," he quickly adapted to the rigors as well as the satisfactions of university life. In 1927, at the end of his freshman year, he was elected to the business board of the campus newspaper, the *Daily Princetonian*. He was a member of the football squad, and in his junior year, he joined the school's polo team. For many years, Marcy had been interested in this sport and hoped that Hartley would follow suit; he even built a polo field on his Spring Valley Road property in Harding Township. Hartley also received a commission as a second lieutenant in the Reserve Officers Training Corps (ROTC) Field Artillery. Gerrie visited him often, and the two grew very close during these years. She would regularly be driven to the university to lunch with him at the Tiger Teapot, a Princeton restaurant, and she warmly welcomed Hartley's friends to Giralda when he brought them home for weekends.[5]

In 1929, just before his senior year, Hartley spent six weeks completing a course in military science and tactics at Princeton. By August, he was ready to take some time off, so he sailed to the West Indies on his yacht with Raymond Patterson, Gerrie's secretary, and two of his Princeton classmates. Like his mother in her early years, he was curious and adventurous—wanting to experience the joys of travel. And so in 1930, after graduating from Princeton and completing yet another round of military training, he decided to tour Europe before beginning graduate school, this time at Columbia University. Anxious to distract him from his interest in flying, Gerrie suggested that Hartley visit various kennels in order to purchase dogs for Giralda, but he was not at all enthusiastic about the idea. Instead it was decided that he would go on a sightseeing trip in his new motorcar.[6]

"Very hectic trying to get Hartley ready," Gerrie noted in her diary on July 20. Two days later, he and a classmate and polo teammate, Ralph W. Applegate of Kansas City, Missouri, set sail for England on the *Transylvania*. Together they motored through

Marcellus Hartley Dodge, Jr., 1928 (Courtesy of Nicolas W. Platt)

England, Scotland, and Ireland, then crossed the English Channel
and headed for Paris. There, on August 28, they dined at the
Hotel Crillon with the manager of that internationally known
establishment, Henri DeQuis (also a Dodge family friend), and
with Ray Patterson, who was en route to Munich to purchase
dogs for Gerrie. With Hartley at the wheel, the two young men
drove out of Paris the next day, in very hot weather. At about 2:30
p.m., as they were about to reach Magesq on the road between

Bordeaux and Bayonne, the car crashed into a gnarled oak tree. Hartley was killed.[7]

Monsieur DeQuis was the first to be notified, and he left immediately for Magesq. As soon as word of the tragic event reached Patterson in Munich, he hurried back to Paris and then went to the scene of the accident. He inspected the wreck and interviewed two young residents of the area, Paul Theo Odin and Andre Dupin, who, along with the chief of the local fire department, a Monsieur Bernadet, had retrieved Hartley's body and saved the badly injured Ralph Applegate from the blazing car, at considerable personal risk. Patterson concluded that Hartley had died instantly, and indeed, that he never had a chance: the entire front of the car was demolished, and the engine had been propelled through the cowling and into the driver's seat.

Patterson also learned that after rescuing Applegate, Odin and Dupin had gone to Dax, the nearest large town, to find a physician, Dr. Destouesse, who went right to the scene, gave the unconscious Applegate first aid, and transferred him to the Riberol Clinic in Dax. Although he had sustained head injuries, a fractured leg, and contusions over his entire body, the young man would recover. But he remained for some time in a state of shock, with no memory of the details of what had happened. The report that appeared in the *Madison (New Jersey) Eagle* asserted that an investigation by the French police did not determine who had been driving at the time of the accident. But in fact, a French police report issued the day after the crash identified Hartley as the driver. The cause of the accident has never been determined.[8]

News of the tragedy reached Giralda late on the day of the accident, and as might be expected, the aftermath was dreadful. Father John Laffey, a Catholic chaplain who was a family friend and happened to be visiting from Illinois at the time, did what he could to comfort Gerrie and Marcy. Family members also tried to help. Gerrie's sister, Emma, was with the couple at Giralda the next day, and noted in her diary that it had been a "day of sadness and great sympathy" for both Dodges. For several days thereafter, she continued to visit in an attempt to help her sister weather the crisis of a lifetime.[9]

Gerrie's diary entries, particularly during these years, were usually rather brief and unemotional. Yet eerily, on August 29, before learning of the disaster, she wrote that she "felt so depressed." The next day, it appears, she went back to that entry to add, "Hartley instantly killed today." The next few days were filled with telephone calls, telegrams, and sympathetic visitors, but there was little anyone could do to assuage the grief of parents who had just been told that their only child was dead.[10]

On September 4, Ray Patterson escorted Hartley's body onto the French liner *Ile de France*, bound for New York. Six days later, family and friends assembled at the Fourteenth Street pier and met the ship. Hartley had been dressed in the uniform of a second lieutenant in the ROTC Field Artillery. A group of his Princeton polo teammates served as his pallbearers, led by U.S. Army captains W. C. Lattimore and R. W. Hasbrouck. In keeping with tradition, before the flag-draped casket touched American soil, Lattimore removed the flag and replaced it with a regulation Army flag. Nearby stood Harry Thoman, the veteran stableman who had served the William Rockefellers from 1899 to 1907, when he moved to Giralda to work for the Dodges. He had known Hartley since he was born and, as noted, had spent countless hours riding with the boy. That sad day was Thoman's fifty-ninth birthday.[11]

The somber entourage moved on to the Dodges' Fifth Avenue residence. There the next morning, last rites were offered by the Reverend Victor W. Mori, pastor of Madison's Grace Episcopal Church, who had officiated at Hartley's confirmation several years earlier. Then a police-escorted, quarter-mile-long funeral procession formed and motored to Sleepy Hollow Cemetery, where Hartley's body was interred in a plot near the family mausoleum. U.S. Army bugler Thomas Carney sounded taps as the casket was lowered into its final resting place.[12]

Gerrie's terse diary entries for the rest of the year reveal her attempt to continue her activities despite her terrible loss. "Very hard days," she noted on November 12. On November 29, she wrote that she "couldn't sleep and felt [I] could not go to Boston," as she had planned. There are few entries for the rest of the year, and no mention of Christmas, which had been such an important holiday for the family every year. On December 13, she noted that she was "busy closing the house."[13]

The events of 1930 left their mark. Understandably, Hartley's death was a tragedy from which neither Gerrie nor Marcy would ever completely recover. Each of them tried to deal with the overwhelming grief, and each emerged as a very different person. Gerrie had begun her life and her marriage as a product of a Gilded Age upbringing—as a sociable young society matron. She had enjoyed luncheons, dinners, theater events, and parties. Marcy had been the quieter, more introspective partner—the hardworking industrialist. According to Mary Jane Ellis, who became Gerrie's companion later in life, these characteristics seemed to reverse after young Hartley died. Gerrie began "to bury herself in her work, while Mr. Dodge seemed to want to go out in society more and more." Marcy began to join clubs in Morris County and Manhattan and to entertain guests, particularly at Hartley Farms. He became warmer and more sociable. Gerrie grew increasingly practical, while indulging more and more in activities that could be enjoyed alone, such as playing the organ she and Marcy had installed at Giralda and listening to opera broadcasts on Saturday afternoons by herself.[14]

Because of this divergence of interests and temperament, unfounded rumors began to circulate that the couple had separated. It was true that they owned two homes and enjoyed different interests, but their basic concern for each other remained strong, even though at times it might be characterized as resembling the kind found in a brother-sister relationship. Marcy's house, originally intended as a future home for Hartley, continued to be maintained as an office and adjunct social space. When Gerrie was out of town, Marcy would stay there and entertain his close friends. Among those friends in later years were Mamie and Dwight Eisenhower, who often stayed the weekend at

Hartley's house during Eisenhower's tenure as president of Columbia University in the late 1940s. But when Gerrie would return to Giralda from visits to New York, Marcy was always there to greet her. It was a marriage of mutual affection, both before and after the death of their son, and it continued to be so until Marcy died in 1963.[15]

That is not to say that Marcy was always a willing participant in activities at Giralda. In the morning, while attending to his business at his office in the carriage house at Hartley Farms, he would ask what was on the lunch menu at Giralda. If he couldn't get the information, or if the meal plan didn't suit him, he would have a member of the Hartley Farms staff make a sandwich for him, which he hid in his pocket. Mary Jane Ellis recalled that after being seated, if he was unhappy about the entree, he would peer around the table's large floral centerpiece, see if Gerrie was watching, and then take the sandwich out and eat it. According to Ellis, although Gerrie knew exactly what he was doing, she "never let on, but she would wink marvelously. . . . She let him have his fun, let him think he had gotten away with it. He fed his main meal to the dogs."[16]

Both Dodges, Ellis maintained, had mischievous senses of humor, and both were capable of humoring each other. For instance, when there were occasions that Marcy wanted to entertain visitors whose interests Gerrie didn't share, he would call her from his Hartley Farms office to report that he had a terrible cold and that he'd better stay the night there rather than come home and pass it on to her. Gerrie would concur, hang up, and announce, "Daddy's going to have a party tonight." She never spoiled his fun.[17]

# CHAPTER IV

# "THE DOG FANCIER
## OF THE CENTURY"

During the 1920s, as Giralda Farms grew and developed, it became home to many kinds of animals. Mallard ducks and Canada geese swam in the Giralda pond. Deer roamed the property, and Arabian horses, Welsh and Shetland ponies, Sardinian donkeys, Toggenburg goats, and pheasants also inhabited the estate. But Gerrie's main focus was on her dogs—a preoccupation that led her to a challenging and rewarding career as a breeder and as a judge at dog shows nationwide as well as in Canada, England, Ireland, and Germany.[1]

During her first few years at Giralda, in deference to her father's wishes, Gerrie did not actively pursue this interest. William felt the estate was better suited to the raising of horses—an interest that appealed more to Marcy. But then, near the end of her father's life, his opposition appeared to fade as he began to appreciate the seriousness and zeal of Gerrie's love for canines. Eventually, Giralda Farms became known both nationally and internationally as the home of the finest breeds. Over the course of the nearly four decades during which Gerrie was committed to this pursuit, 180 Giralda dogs became champions and obedience winners in various events, and more than 200 won the title "Best in Show." Ultimately, Geraldine Rockefeller Dodge came to be known as the "first lady of dogdom" and "the dog fancier of the century."[2]

Gerrie had been passionate about dogs ever since her father presented her with her first English terrier, when she was six years old. She seemed to understand them in ways that others around her could not. In adulthood, she found a particularly compelling explanation for her special relationship with dogs in the 1954 book *Kinship with All Life*, written by J. Allen Boone, a student of human-animal relationships. Discussing the animal-human bond generally, Boone noted the reassurance and peace of mind that could be found in "companionship beyond the boundaries of humanity." Those who relate best to animals, he observed, are able to share such "assets" as love, enthusiasm, loyalty, and other values with lesser species. He saw this connection as stretching back to an ancient time when "the whole earth was of one language and speech . . . and all was one grand concord." Drawn to these ideas, Gerrie owned a copy of Boone's book and made frequent reference to it.[3]

To understand this philosophy and Gerrie's interest in it is to grasp the vital role that her pets played in her life as the years progressed. Naturally, she could and did hire numerous people to tend the dogs in her kennels. Yet she also spent much of her own time feeding and caring for them. And when dogs died, she had them buried in a specially designated area of the estate, their graves marked with custom-made headstones.

## KENNELS AT GIRALDA FARMS

In 1913 Gerrie bought a German shepherd named Hyphen and decided to breed her. Unfortunately, this first attempt did not result in a litter of healthy dogs. But within the next few years, she was successful enough to rival the most prominent American pioneer in the breed, P. A. B. Widener of Elkins Park, Pennsylvania. Early on, she recognized the importance of employing a first-rate kennel manager, and she found him in A. McClure ("Mac") Halley, who began traveling abroad to find and buy the best examples of breeds for Giralda. In October 1922 Gerrie's German police dog

Kix von Oeringen took top prizes at shows in Tuxedo, New York, and Englewood, New Jersey. In addition to winning awards for her own dogs, she began to establish a reputation as a judge, becoming in 1924 the first woman to serve in that capacity at the famed Westminster Kennel Club Show in New York City, where she was asked to judge Best in Show. In the same year, she hosted an event at Giralda for nearly four hundred dog fanciers to view eleven of the best shepherd dogs to be found in Europe and America, several of which were owned by the Giralda Farms kennels, P. A. B. Widener, and other breeders.[4]

In 1924 as well, Gerrie acquired Giralda Schatz von Hoehentann from a breeder in the Bavarian Alps; he was picked as Best of Breed at many important dog shows, including the above-mentioned 1924 Westminster event. Indeed, he was referred to in canine circles that year as "the most talked about dog in the country." In 1925 another of her shepherds, Giralda Teuthilde von Hagenheiss, was judged the best dog of any breed at the National Dog Show in Cincinnati, having won first honors at ten successive exhibitions around the country. This pattern continued, as other dogs were brought to Giralda, conditioned and groomed, and then entered in shows throughout the United States.[5]

Gerrie's concentration on German shepherds revealed her interest not only in their breeding but also in their history and in progressive methods of care. She wanted them to be trained to be alert, affectionate companions as well as effective watchdogs. She developed a course, which she carefully followed and constantly found ways to improve. On a rotating basis, dogs were admitted into her own home for a period, during which they were taught to develop the kind of self-control and discipline that would enable them to be house pets as well as show dogs. She even converted a window in her bedroom into a trapdoor, connected to a ramp leading to her kennels, so that the dogs could enter and exit without passing through the main house. One sign of the sort of kinship Gerrie developed with the dogs trained in her house was that they often became rather protective of her. Years later, her

"Mac's Folly," the 1936 Fleetwood Cadillac named for A. McClure Halley
(Courtesy of St. Hubert's Giralda)

longtime butler Ernest Barton reportedly "got the seat of his
pants taken off a few times when he would bring Mrs. Dodge
her evening snack." [6]

The Giralda kennels covered almost four acres and held up
to 150 dogs, with several resident overseers in charge. As early as
1924, the facilities were described as "nothing short of palatial,"
with yards that "must be the envy of all dog owners who visit
this estate." The kennels were hosed down twice a day, and the
dogs were kept scrupulously clean and given plenty of exercise.
They were provided with the best food—usually round steak and
vegetables on a bed of shredded wheat or kibble—and with a
continuous source of fresh drinking water. Breeding sections
were set aside, as were areas for bitches and their newborn litters.
When old enough to walk, puppies were moved to parts of the
buildings where they could receive sunlight and have room to dig,
play, and develop. Giralda dogs traveled to shows in a specially
equipped Fleetwood Cadillac, which is said to have held twelve

canines comfortably. Dogs returning from shows were quarantined so that any diseases they might have picked up would not be transmitted. In short, the kennels at Giralda Farms and those Mrs. Dodge also established during this period at Princeton, New Jersey—administered under the direction of the renowned obedience trainer, John Simmons—became the ultimate ideal for dog fanciers everywhere.[7]

The Giralda kennels also became widely renowned as a source for the finest dogs that could be bred. Dog fanciers from throughout the world visited Giralda to purchase German shepherds, and, eventually, pointers and English cocker spaniels. In 1924, for instance, the Maharajah of Jind, an Indian potentate, arrived in New York City for a visit and immediately told his aide-de-camp to locate the best shepherd dogs in the area. The American Kennel Club directed him to Giralda Farms, and the maharajah came to see its remarkable canines and take a tour of its splendid training facilities. Duly impressed, he offered $10,000 to acquire one of Gerrie's finest German shepherds, Ch. Iso von Doernerhof. Gerrie politely but firmly refused, since she did not want to sell the dog at any price. She offered him another one, at a comparatively low price, but he turned her down. "I am just as glad that he did not buy a dog," she remarked. "I would hate to see one of my dogs go to India. It is so far away." What she meant was that it would be difficult to check up on the dog's progress from such a distance.

Indeed, as her companion in later years, Mary Jane Ellis, recalled, selling a dog did not end Gerrie's relationship with the animal or with its new owner; she was scrupulous about following their progress. In most cases, she was satisfied with the reports. Sometimes, however, she was disappointed. An extreme situation occurred with Kerry, an English cocker spaniel Gerrie sold to a Florida woman who failed to care for him. After being notified that he had become homeless, she sent for him, restored his health from the "bag of bones" he had become, and then entered him in the 1947 American Spaniel Club Specialty Show held at the Hotel Roosevelt in New York; Kerry took all blue ribbons as Best of Breed. When Father John Laffey purchased a German shepherd from Gerrie and did not keep her posted about its welfare, Ellis recalled, he "got a hot letter from her saying she wanted to know how the dog was coming on." His reply began what was to become a regular communication between them—and a special friendship. During trips east from his home in Illinois, Father Laffey was a frequent visitor at Giralda.[8]

Between 1937 and 1942, the English cocker spaniel became Gerrie's most successful breed. Recognizing the differences in the characteristics of the English and American types, she decided to mount an educational campaign, the ultimate goal of which was to separate the breeds. In recognition of her dedicated efforts, she was elected to the presidency of the English Cocker Spaniel Club of America in 1942 and, the same year, published a book, *The English Cocker Spaniel in America*. In 1946, largely due to her research and efforts, a new American standard for cocker spaniels was established, which in turn led to the official separation of the two breeds. In 1956, with her research assistant, Josephine Z. Rine, she authored a second book, *The German Shepherd Dog in America*.[9]

Gerrie also believed that more research was needed to improve the health of dogs and to treat the diseases afflicting them. Therefore, in 1950 she was most interested to learn that the Cornell University Research Laboratories for Diseases of Dogs (in 1975 renamed the James A. Baker Institute for Animal Health) intended to build a new laboratory on the Cornell campus in Ithaca, New York; its purpose would be to study ways to reduce the great number of disease-related canine deaths that were then occurring. When Gerrie was invited to help in its establishment, she responded by underwriting one section of the facility, which subsequently became known as the Giralda Division. Here the first tissue-culture laboratory in any veterinary college in the world was established, and key discoveries took place. These included the development of vaccines through cell-culture studies rather than by the less humane method of using live animals for experiments.[10]

After hosting educational and specialty shows of the German
Shepherd Dog Club of America in the mid-1920s, Gerrie, along
with Ray Patterson, Carroll B. Merritt, and others established
the Morris and Essex Kennel Club, with the idea of promoting
purebred dogs and sponsoring competitions. In 1927 they staged
the first Morris and Essex Kennel Club Dog Show, held on the
polo field Marcy had built for young Hartley, with New Jersey
Governor A. Harry Moore and his wife among the hundreds in
attendance. About six hundred dogs were entered, representing
seventeen breeds; a panel of prominent judges evaluated them.
The show was a great success and became an annual event, held
on the fourth Saturday in May.[11]

By 1929, Madison residents were beginning to understand
the impact that the show was having on the borough and its
economy. It was becoming common to hear the refrain, "Judges,
exhibitors, dog owners and lovers, guests of the notable hospitality
of Mrs. Dodge, will not soon forget Madison." Indeed, the quickly
growing fame of the show also made it possible for Gerrie to
attract Captain Max von Stephanitz, developer of the German
shepherd breed in Germany in 1899 and author of *The German
Shepherd in Word and Pictures*—then known as the bible of
German shepherd fanciers—to serve as a judge in 1930. Von
Stephanitz evaluated all the dogs entered for such qualities as
character, proportion, angulation, body, head, and gait. His arrival
was important to Mrs. Dodge, who, as Edwin J. Sayres, Sr., president of St. Hubert's Giralda, recalled, "valued the opinions of the
European judges because, after all, the majority of breeds origi-
nated there. These people had great history and background and
their opinions meant a great deal." Beginning in 1930, the year
after she and Marcy purchased the neighboring Harkness property,
Gerrie was able to house a number of the judges right on the
estate; the rest she accommodated in area hotels.[12]

Gerrie presents a trophy for Best in Show at the Morris and Essex Kennel Club
Dog Show, 1930 (Courtesy of the Madison Public Library)

The Morris and Essex Kennel Club show became the largest
of its kind in the world and certainly the most prestigious in the
United States. The first year in which registration soared was
1931, when the popular movie dog Rin Tin Tin put in an appearance. Thereafter, the entry list increased, the prizes became more
extravagant, and the crowds grew ever larger. By 1936, "See you
at Madison!" seemed to be the annual exclamation of dog fanciers
nationwide and even abroad. It was not only the largest but also
the most fashionable, the *Madison Eagle* noted that year. And,
more than any other local project or event, it had put Madison on
the map. The peak year was 1939, when 4,456 dogs were regis-
tered, 83 breeds were represented and judged, and 50,000 people
attended. Over the years, more and more people arrived in cars.

Gerrie with the famous German shepherd Rin Tin Tin, who was brought to the Morris and
Essex Club Kennel Club Dog Show in 1931 (Courtesy of St. Hubert's Giralda)

By 1953, Gerrie found it necessary to set aside an additional 20 acres of her property for parking, bringing the total event area to about 130 acres, including 3½ acres completely under tents so attendees could be protected from sun or rain—more canvas than can be seen at the largest circuses. There was even a field hospital, staffed by a doctor and two nurses and serviced by five ambulances. In all, the show required about 750 in staff, including 125 policemen.[13]

From 1942 through 1945, the Morris and Essex Kennel Club Dog Show was suspended because of wartime shortages and restrictions. It resumed in 1946, and even though the number of breeds entered was now down to 30, it was still the world's largest one-day dog show and remained so, drawing in leading canine specialists as judges and attracting big crowds.[14]

It also was a grand social occasion, with no expense spared. Gerrie provided transportation for participants to and from the Madison railroad station. Her butler Ernest Barton recalled that on the eve of each show, she hosted a glittering reception and supper, provided by a leading New York caterer, with all guests properly announced and received at the front door. The next morning, Gerrie would arrive at the grounds, welcome visitors, and take part in the activities. For guests and judges, elegant food would be served at beautifully appointed tables; for the general public, there were food stands staffed by volunteers. Gerrie was the grand dame of the Morris and Essex show. The fact that it ran into the red each year due to the extravagant level of her entertaining and accommodations didn't matter; the entire undertaking was a labor of love.[15]

In 1954 the Morris and Essex show was suspended when the American Kennel Club decided to host its own show on the same weekend; the Madison event resumed the next year. In October 1958, with her energy on the wane, Gerrie announced the show's permanent suspension. Officially, she explained that there had been a rise in the number of outdoor dog shows nationally and that they might be expected to carry on in the tradition of the Morris and Essex.[16]

Aerial view of the Morris and Essex Kennel Club
Dog Show, Hartley Farms, 1938
(Courtesy of St. Hubert's Giralda)

The Morris and Essex Kennel Club Dog Show, Hartley Farms, about 1939 (Courtesy of St. Hubert's Giralda).

E
HOUNDS
GIRALDA FARMS

Gerrie and Marcy at the Morris and Essex Kennel Club Dog Show, 1946
(Courtesy of St. Hubert's Giralda)


### ST. HUBERT'S GIRALDA

One day in 1915, while the Dodges were still living on Spring
Valley Road, Gerrie's little dog Sam, who was in the daily habit
of following Marcy's car to the Madison railroad station, didn't
return home. After looking everywhere she could, Gerrie posted
notices throughout the area, offered a $50 reward for Sam's
return, and even hired detectives to track him down. When the
dog was found, having been taken in as a stray, she was over-
joyed. She had occasionally adopted strays of her own; after all,
Giralda was named for the patron saint of orphans, and to Gerrie,
dogs qualified.[17]

Over the years, Gerrie grew increasingly aware of the needs
of strays and other such dogs that were far less fortunate than
the ones she owned. In 1939 she established St. Hubert's Giralda,
an animal-welfare organization named for the sixth-century bishop
of Liège and apostle of Adrennes and Brabant. (St. Hubert is the

patron saint of huntsmen, and because his descendants have been said to possess the power to cure rabies, he is also considered to be the patron saint of dogs.) Gerrie served as the organization's president and treasurer from the year it was founded until 1964. The shelter had at its disposal three radio-equipped ambulances, animal wardens, and additional staff to patrol Madison and its environs in order to locate and retrieve sick, injured, and stray dogs.[18]

After ending the Morris and Essex show in 1958, Gerrie focused increasingly on St. Hubert's, noting, "To this unhappy segment of dogdom, I now give top priority of my time and strength." The same year, she set aside sixteen acres of Giralda Farms to build an animal shelter and an education center for St. Hubert's. Wanting "these unfortunate animals to be comfortable," and practicing what she preached, she spent a good deal of time at the new facility and continued occasionally adopting some of the strays and orphans herself.[19]

## AWARDS

Gerrie's abiding love of dogs and her animal welfare activities brought her public attention and numerous awards. In 1951, as a result of a poll conducted in 1950 by the American Kennel Club, she and Alfred M. Dick of Philadelphia, the American Kennel Club's field representative, received awards as dogdom's woman and man of the year. That same year, for the third year in a row, Gerrie was named "Dogdom's Woman of the Year" by the Gaines Research Center. In 1951 she also won the Quaker Oats award "for distinguished service to American dogdom." And in 1954, Giralda Farms was awarded the Fido—seen in dog circles as the equivalent of Hollywood's Oscar—in recognition of "Giralda's position as the top-winning kennel of the year."[20]

# CHAPTER V

# PHILANTHROPY

*He hath oversoared the shadow of our night,*
*Envy and calumny and hate and pain,*
*And that unrest which men miscall delight.*
*Can touch him not, and torture not again;*
*From the contagion of the world's slow stain,*
*He is secure, and now can never mourn,*
*A heart grown cold, a head grown grey in vain;*
*Nor, where the spirit's self has ceased to burn,*
*With sparkless ashes load an unlamented urn.*

—Percy Bysshe Shelley, *Adonais: An Elegy*
*on the Death of John Keats,* 1821

From May 30, 1935, until the end of her life, one of Geraldine
Rockefeller Dodge's most cherished possessions was a small,
dark-blue, morocco-bound brochure, produced by Tiffany and
Company of New York, that contained a resolution of thanks for
her donation of the Hartley Dodge Memorial, the borough hall
of Madison. It was a beautiful, meticulously scribed document.
But for Gerrie, it was the inclusion of the fortieth stanza of a
late work by the English Romantic poet Percy Bysshe Shelley
(1792–1822) that made the brochure a deeply prized possession.
In 1821 Shelly wrote *Adonais* in memory of his friend the poet
John Keats, who had died the year before. Like her beloved son,
Keats had met a premature end. Both she and Marcy were moved

by the comparison and also by the borough's thoughtfulness in including such meaningful symbolism. The mayor and council pledged to honor Gerrie's wish to create an "enduring and lasting monument to the memory of her son, one which will stand as a perpetual memorial." They also understood her desire to have the building maintained forever "as an expression of true mother love."[1]

If borough attorney Henry G. Pilch and councilman Joseph E. Pooley, who commissioned the brochure, had hesitated over whether to include lines of poetry in their resolution, they would have been reassured if they had seen some of the examples of favorite poems included in Gerrie's papers. An undated and unsigned poem, titled "While I Live," reveals her attitude about charity, nurtured early in life by the example of the Rockefeller family:

> *Since it has been my lot to find*
> *At every parting of the road,*
> *The helping hand of comrade kind,*
> *To assist me with my heavy load:*
> *And since I have no gold to give,*
> *And love alone must make amends,*
> *My humble prayer is, while I live*
> *God make me worthy of my friends.*[2]

Long before 1935, she realized that she did have "gold to give." Among the first local institutions to benefit from her generosity was Morristown Memorial Hospital. In 1921 she donated $50,000 toward construction of a nurses' residence and awarded prizes in memory of her mother, who had recently died, for the best nursing students. And in the same year, she began an unparalleled four-decade period of philanthropy on behalf of the borough of Madison.[3]

In 1920 a fire broke out at Giralda and destroyed a barn. Firemen quickly arrived on the scene and extinguished the blaze, but not without great difficulty. Gerrie realized that the borough's hook-and-ladder as well as the hose company needed better, more

modern equipment. After making appropriate inquiries, she
donated $18,000 for the purchase of an Ahearn Fox Fire Engine.
Capable of throwing 1,300 gallons of water per minute, it was
the best fire-fighting apparatus then available. According to the
resolution signed by sixty-nine firemen and presented to Gerrie
by Mayor William A. Starrett, Madison's fire department was
now "second to none of the towns in this state of like size." The
borough responded to her gift by holding a parade and a dinner
in her honor—hailed in Madison as the "biggest day in history."
But Gerrie's generosity to the fire department did not end there.
In 1949 she helped it purchase a new Mack pumper, and in 1953
she underwrote the entire cost of another one. "I've always considered Madison to be a very lovely home town," she told the
mayor and council at the time, "and I am very proud that the
town fathers have always seen fit to maintain adequate and
up-to-date fire apparatus."[4]

Gerrie also began to expand her generosity according to the
needs of a wide range of individuals and organizations, supply-
ing more or less money, as the situation required. By the early
1920s, having provided for the recreational needs of her own son,
she realized that the children of Madison also needed a modern
playground. In July 1922 she purchased the Condit, Collver, and
Hayes properties on Greenwood Avenue, a four-and-one-half acre
site adjoining the Central Avenue athletic field. Later named
Dodge Field, the total cost for the land, its grading, and installation
of playground facilities and equipment came to about $60,000,
most of it provided by Gerrie. At the same time, she tried to
increase the area of the playground further by offering to raze
the Bethel A. M. E. Church, located on a Central Avenue corner
of the property, and pay for the construction of a new sanctuary
on another site in town. But the congregation was not in favor
of the proposal, and so today the church remains in its original
location.[5]

Gerrie was learning that her efforts weren't always apprecia-
ted. Indeed, she was finding that a few politicians and citizens
of the borough were overly critical of the process used to obtain

bids for the clearing and grading of the field. In an open letter to the *Madison Eagle*, she complained about "grudges and petty politics," noting that she had "borne a great deal of expense to provide a playground" and that she resented what she saw as the petty annoyances related to the development of the property— problems that she believed had discouraged earlier benefactions by others. The paper's editor agreed, saying her latest efforts on the borough's behalf had become "the football of certain small town political fry." Nevertheless, the new playground was completed and formally opened for use in June 1924.[6]

Gerrie also wanted to improve other recreational resources, so in 1925 she provided nets for use on the borough's tennis courts—a donation made through the playground committee of the Thursday Morning Club. Three years later, when tent caterpillars threatened local trees, she sponsored a competition among Madison's public school students to gather egg clusters in order to stop the spread of the destructive insects.[7]

In 1921, Gerrie began to assemble contiguous properties in order to give them to Madison as the site for a new municipal building. Her first purchase was a magnificent tract of land between Green Avenue and Prospect Street, opposite the railroad station and adjacent to the borough center, with frontage of about seven hundred feet on Kings Road. Subsequent legal problems, particularly difficulties presented by her unsuccessful attempts to exercise an option to purchase adjoining property owned by local businessman Alfred P. Smith, threatened to delay or even ultimately prevent the transfer of enough land for the intended purpose. Smith had decided that he did not want to sell the amount of land contained in the option agreement. Gerrie persevered, won a court battle to exercise her full option, and by 1922 had put together an appropriate parcel. At the same time, Mrs. Margaretta V. Webb gave the borough an adjoining bit of acreage on Kings Road and Green Avenue, further expanding the site on which the new municipal building would stand. Gerrie, in turn, purchased an additional large lot at the same intersection, designating it for a park that would enhance the borough hall.[8]

After Hartley's death in 1930, Gerrie began a serious review
of her approach to philanthropy. She was forty-eight years old;
there would be no more children. With no direct heirs to their
vast estate, she and Marcy began pondering the question of its
ultimate disposition, and they made some momentous decisions.
One of their first gifts was made in 1931, on the occasion of the
first reunion of Hartley's Princeton University graduating class:
Marcy announced that the family would underwrite construction
of a memorial archway in Hartley's memory between Pyne and
Henry halls on the quadrangle at Princeton.[9]

But Gerrie, consistent with her habit of civic largesse, also
wanted to memorialize her son appropriately by building an
edifice that would have a lasting effect on the quality of life in
Madison. She concluded that the planned municipal building,
intended to unite all branches of borough government under one
roof for the first time, could be named for her son. Although she
and Margaretta Webb had already provided an appropriate parcel
of land, Gerrie decided to underwrite the entire cost of the building's construction as well and to provide an endowment for its
upkeep. By any reckoning, it was the sort of gift rarely given by
an individual to a municipality.[10]

With Madison officials and citizens delighted by the
prospect of this singular donation, Gerrie engaged the Summit,
New Jersey, architectural firm of Richard S. Shapter to provide
the plans. She had known Shapter for at least a decade, since he
had designed her townhouse at 800 Fifth Avenue in New York,
and she was confident that he would be capable of achieving the
monumentality she envisioned for the borough hall. A colonial-
style building with a columned portico seemed most appropriate,
she believed. Shapter responded with the design for the magnificent and substantial two-story structure that stands today, 216
feet wide by 65 feet deep. The center section, situated between
two broad wings, is dominated by a Greek Revival facade with
six thirty-foot-tall marble Doric columns set on bases measuring
three feet in diameter. The Vermont-green slate roof is set off by
a marble cupola that includes a bronze belfry. A lightning-rod-

topped weather vane brings the building's height to 120 feet.[11]

The building is sheathed in fireproof structural steel and stone; the interior is likewise composed of fine and enduring materials. Granite from quarries at West Chelmsford, Massachusetts, rare Westland marble (no longer commercially quarried at the time), and black Belgian marble were used, along with bronze for doors and railings and red Honduras mahogany for interior finishes. Besides fully underwriting the construction costs, Gerrie paid for all the interior furnishings— the total adding up to some $800,000. She also pledged $300,000, to be paid over three years, as an endowment for structural repairs, a promise she fulfilled only six months after the building's dedication in 1935.[12]

Ground was broken on September 13, 1932, and excavation began at the end of October. Gerrie, whom a recently passed borough ordinance had granted "full and complete" authority over construction, had studied various bids before choosing the New York City firm of William Crawford as general contractor. The same firm had overseen construction of her Manhattan townhouse in 1922 and, back in 1886, of John D. Rockefeller's Pocantico Hills estate.[13]

Gerrie insisted that the work force consist of as many Madison residents as possible—except where those in a given trade, such as steelworking, were locally unavailable. The country was then in the depths of the paralyzing Great Depression, and she was anxious to relieve the borough's unemployment problems. Because of her insistence, many men, particularly bricklayers and masons, were thus able to stay off the borough's relief rolls during construction. And, through the mayor's Emergency Employment Committee, a rotation was set up that enabled a number of people to obtain at least temporary employment on the project. In addition, Gerrie provided as much work as she could for Madison residents at Giralda Farms.[14]

The building was completed in the spring of 1935, with formal dedication ceremonies held, fittingly enough, on May 30—Memorial Day. Some two thousand spectators packed Kings

Gerrie and Marcy at the dedication of the Hartley Dodge Memorial, 1935. Father John Laffey is at the podium. (Courtesy of St. Hubert's Giralda)

Road, between the new structure and the railroad station. County Judge Albert H. Holland, Mrs. Dodge's attorney, presided, and Father John Laffey, the Catholic priest who had comforted the Dodges when Hartley died, delivered the invocation. He spoke movingly of Hartley, as:

> *the lad in whose honor this building comes to an understanding city, passed out of this sphere in his early manhood, on the threshold of a life of great usefulness. And from out the wreckage and frustrated hopes that his passing entailed rises this edifice, a sermon in stone on how to bear the cross; on how to carry on for God and country in the face of any sorrow even the most devastating, and the most perplexing.*

New Jersey's senior U.S. Senator, W. Warren Barbour, stood up to praise Gerrie's generosity and dedication. Other speakers

The Hartley Dodge Memorial on the day of its dedication, 1935
(Courtesy of St. Hubert's Giralda)

included Luther P. Eisenhart, Hartley's faculty advisor at Princeton,
who referred to him as "a delightful companion to persons of any
age, ever ready to help others no matter at what inconvenience
to himself." Judge Holland returned to the platform to say, "Like a
handclasp forever warm, this memorial expresses as nothing else
could your feeling for your departed son." He then introduced
Gerrie, who formally submitted to Mayor Alan H. Brown the
document that legally transferred the structure to the borough.
After the benediction, offered by the Reverend Victor W. Mori
of Madison's Grace Episcopal Church, the Dodges hosted a buffet
luncheon for six hundred public officials and friends at the former
Harkness mansion adjoining Giralda Farms.[15]

There were yet more celebrations. Local firemen honored
Gerrie in July, presenting her with a resolution of appreciation
for the amenities provided for them in the new building, which
included a dormitory, bathroom facilities, and a fully-equipped
social room. As she accepted their thanks, she was given a
tremendous ovation. Firemen broke into song, with everyone

Beatrice Longman
(American 1874–1954)
Marcellus Hartley Dodge, Jr.,
about 1926
This presently unlocated marble
bas relief was the source for the
bronze plaque installed in the
lobby of the Hartley Dodge
Memorial. (Courtesy of the
Madison Public Library)

joining in the strains of "Auld Lang Syne." It was a night of good fellowship and fun. Marcy even claimed $10 from his wife after winning a bet that he could slide down the fire pole.[16]

On July 29, 1936—Hartley's twenty-eighth birthday and a year after the building opened—grateful Madison borough employees initiated an annual ceremony, one that continues to the present day. They placed flowers in front of the memorial plaque to Hartley, located in the building's lobby.[17]

Encouraged by the community's warm appreciation, Gerrie continued to be interested in the Hartley Dodge Memorial after construction was completed. In 1939 she underwrote the cost of a sprinkler system for the property's lawn and, in 1956, provided funds to install air-conditioning units throughout the building. She paid great attention as well to the interior appointments.

In 1938 she donated a portrait of herself, painted in Europe in
1906 by the noted German artist Friedrich August von Kaulbach;
it was hung in the council chamber, directly behind the mayor's
chair. (Local legend has it that she wanted it placed there so she
could oversee the proceedings in perpetuity.) She also donated a
beautiful rug for the mayor's office and two Gobelin tapestries
for the council chamber walls.[18]

In April 1942 Gerrie presented a group of important artworks
to grace the building further. There was a late-eighteenth-century
bronze bust of Benjamin Franklin by the French sculptor Jean-
Antoine Houdon (1741–1828); mid-nineteenth-century portraits
of George and Martha Washington by Rembrandt Peale (1778–
1860); and other portraits from the same period by Bass Otis
(1784–1861) of Henry Clay and by George Peter Alexander Healy
(1813–1894) of John Quincy Adams. The gift also included a
late-nineteenth-century marble likeness of Napoleon by Auguste
Rodin (1840–1917) and a twentieth-century bronze bust of
Abraham Lincoln by Max Bachmann (1862–1921).

Additionally, Gerrie donated a large William F. K. Travers
(1828–1882) portrait of Lincoln, completed at the end of the
Civil War, that she had only recently managed to secure from
her brother Percy's estate; it had hung in his Manhattan office.
In presenting that painting, she noted with evident emotion that
"ever since this building was built, it was my desire to have that
Lincoln portrait . . . here." Perhaps she was aware of the importance of the work, which Ward Hill Lamon, a close friend of the
sixteenth president, had called "the most lifelike picture of Mr.
Lincoln I have ever seen on canvas." Also depicted in the painting
is an unattributed bust of George Washington and *Washington
Crossing the Delaware* (1851), by the renowned history painter
Emanuel Leutze (1816–1868)—both undoubtedly incorporated
to document the use of Washington's image as additional inspiration for Lincoln's effort to save the Union.

Accepting the gifts for the borough, Mayor Samuel A. Gruver
told Mrs. Dodge, "These . . . great works of art should and will
help to furnish us all with the inspiration and courage we need

in these troublous (*sic*) times." Dr. Arlo A. Brown, president of
nearby Drew University, followed up by pointing out that the
"debunking and playing down of heroes a few years ago had a
great deal to do with leading the world to the state it is now in,
and this showing of heroes can do much to bring the world back
to order." These officials' remarks had a direct meaning. America
had entered World War II just a few months earlier, and many
of Madison's young men were serving in Europe and Asia;
thirty-eight would not return.[19]

In April 1950, Gerrie's decades-long pattern of generosity to
the borough was recognized with a glittering testimonial dinner.
Speaking at the occasion, Drew University president Fred C.
Holloway noted the similarity between this gathering and the
citywide demonstrations of appreciation held for Giotto in
Florence whenever that late-medieval Italian master completed
a new painting. Noting that Mrs. Dodge's contributions to the
community came under seven headings—protection, health,
convenience, youth, reputation of the borough, beauty, and
personality—he emphasized that a significant number of her
charitable acts had been unknown except to their recipients,
as they were accomplished with no publicity or fanfare. A few
months later, Mayor Norman J. Griffiths characterized the
testimonial as "a long overdue tribute to a most gracious and
understanding American lady." There were more such accolades.
In 1953 Gerrie shared the Rotary Club's annual "leading citizen"
award with Robert C. B. Parker, the retiring borough superintendent of schools.[20]

Gerrie's response to these tributes was simply to continue
her generosity. Only two weeks after the 1950 testimonial dinner,
it was announced that she would deed a large piece of property
at the corner of Madison Avenue and Morris Street to be used as
a site for an additional large water tank that would reinforce the
borough's water system. And in 1958, after it had been determined that Madison needed a new YMCA building, she donated
the former Lackawanna freight station property, a site comprising
more than six acres, for that purpose. The original YMCA on

Main Street had accommodated fewer than two hundred members when it was built in 1908. By 1958 membership had risen to more than fifteen hundred—women and girls as well as men and boys. Also, in 1961 she granted use of a parcel of her land on Maple Street for erection of the Ambulance Corps building.[21]

In addition to her land donations in Madison, in 1948 Gerrie made a formal presentation of six-and-one-quarter acres in Parsippany-Troy Hills, New Jersey, as the site for a new municipal building that is still in use today.[22]

Both Dodges also were generous to various religious organizations, especially Grace Episcopal Church in Madison. Interviewed in 1976, the Reverend William Nieman noted the difference between the kinds of gifts Gerrie and Marcy gave, thereby revealing their individual approaches to philanthropy during those years. Marcy, said the clergyman, was more interested in steam pipes, parking lots, and storm windows, while Gerrie was concerned with the decorating, enlarging, and overall appearance of the church itself. In 1959, in memory of her son Hartley, she presented the church with a stained-glass window depicting St. Francis of Assisi with the wolf of Gubbio. She took a great interest in the window while it was being made. According to the Reverend Nieman, she apparently wanted "the wild dog standing next to St. Francis [to] look something like her own favorite German shepherd."[23]

Although Gerrie was quite generous, it was not as though any organization requesting help would receive a check. On one notable occasion in the late 1950s, during a visit to the Hartley Dodge Memorial, she was asked to provide a new oven for the firemen's quarters. Kneeling down to the level of the oven, she reached into the appliance, felt some grease, and then responded to the request by offering to donate twenty-five cents to purchase oven cleaner! She was constantly faced with choices. Especially during her later years, she was barraged with written requests for money. Her companion Mary Jane Ellis recalled that Gerrie read every one of the letters, and when a particular hard-luck story would catch her imagination, she would send a trusted

Gerrie out for a ride in a carriage pulled by her champion Welsh stallion, "Mastershot," 1947 (Courtesy of St. Hubert's Giralda)

representative to investigate. In many cases, after hearing his report, she would make arrangements to provide help. Anonymously, she paid mortgages, and before Christmas each year, she would routinely scan the newspapers for articles describing the holiday season's neediest citizens, so that she could help them.[24]

Despite her enormous wealth, she had an acute understanding of the value of money and expected the same of others. On occasion, she would lend money to employees, expect them to repay her, and then, after they had done so, return the money to them if she thought they had truly understood and willingly accepted their responsibility. Inevitably, there were loans that were not repaid, but even those stories occasionally had an interesting twist. For instance, in 1924 and 1925 she had loaned

$2,400 to a cousin, Ernest Johnson. Years passed, and she heard
nothing from him. Then one day in early October 1951, an enve-
lope arrived at Giralda Farms containing a letter and a check
to Gerrie for $6,252. Apologizing for the quarter-century delay,
Ernest explained that the large sum represented the amount
borrowed plus interest, figured at six percent, from January 1,
1925, to October 1, 1951. Gerrie's next move was typical of her,
but to Ernest highly unexpected. She wrote to thank him for the
payment but added, "The loan was made with the idea of helping
you rather than for any financial benefits that I might sustain
from it. Therefore I really do not feel that I could accept the
$3,852 interest. So I am returning your check, and if you will
forward me one for $2,400 I would feel well compensated as it
has helped you when you needed it and that has gratified me
very much."

Replying, Ernest freely admitted that he did not know exactly
what to do. He wondered if he should "continue insisting that
I pay the interest or . . . acquiesce with the thoughts in your
letter." He decided to send a check for the $2,400 with the hope
that Gerrie would "in the near future, let me discuss with you
my thoughts relative to the interest due."

Gerrie responded by thanking him again and assuring him
that "I am glad that this is the exception that proves the rule is
not infallible—never make a loan to a friend or you lose the
friend." Such was her constant dilemma: the desire to be of help
while at the same time recognizing, as she said to Mary Jane Ellis,
that "you never help a person financially and remain a friend."[25]

# CHAPTER VI

# ART

Daily life at Giralda Farms was ordered and predictable. Every employee was assigned specific tasks within a program designed to keep the estate running efficiently. Mary Jane Ellis recalled that, even as she aged, Gerrie would "bounce out of bed" at 7:00 a.m. Her personal maid would then arrive to take the dogs from her quarters. Breakfast was served at 8:00 a.m. on weekdays and Saturday and promptly at 8:30 on Sunday. After breakfast, it was Gerrie's habit to confer with the cook concerning the day's meals and plan menus for the following day. She then went to her office on the second floor of the mansion to receive her estate superintendent's daily report and to tell him anything noteworthy she had observed during her drive around the property the previous day. Her correspondence secretary would then arrive to take dictation, and after that she would meet with her research assistant, Josephine Z. Rine. The morning would conclude with a visit to the kennels, where Gerrie would often exercise the large dogs.[1]

Luncheon was at 1:00 p.m., followed by a meeting with her financial secretary to review invoices. She then went to see how her small dogs were doing and to walk some of them. "Then we'd get in the car and drive around the place," said Ellis. "She'd look at every tree and the deer and what have you. She'd see that everything was in order." The rest of the day was devoted to activities such as feeding carrots to the horses, signing checks, and perhaps dictating more letters. By 5:00 p.m., she would begin catching up on her reading—particularly the day's newspapers. Ellis noted that Gerrie tried to keep herself informed about current events; she expected all around her to do so as well and then to take part intelligently in discussions on topics that interested her. Dinner was at 7:00 p.m., after which she would open mail, make phone calls, and conclude any of the day's unfinished business. She usually retired about 9:00 p.m.[2]

There were several sides to the personality and background of Geraldine Rockefeller Dodge. On the one hand, she was the dog fancier with a soft heart for strays and orphans. On the other, she was a lady of her ancestry and time, legitimately devoted to cultural pursuits related to music and the arts. Ellis remembered that she "never missed listening to the opera over the radio every week, and one didn't disturb her while she was listening." She also enjoyed other musical performances and plays, and felt a desire to be involved generally in the cultural life of New York City. Weekly visits to Manhattan provided a needed break from the routine at Giralda Farms; she would go to the Rockefeller offices at 26 Broadway to see her brother Percy and (after his death in 1934) her nephews in order to handle business affairs. She also would meet friends for lunch and dinner and shop— mainly for antiques and art objects.[3]

It became her habit to go to New York on Tuesday afternoon, staying until Thursday. Her chauffeur would take her directly to her townhouse at Fifth Avenue and Sixty-first Street, a six-story, thirty-five-room modified Georgian Revival-style dwelling designed by the Summit, New Jersey, architect Richard S. Shapter. Completed in 1922, it had formal rooms and other standard appointments, but it also reportedly contained a kennel on the sixth floor. The outbuildings included a garage, chauffeur's quarters, and stables. Gardens graced the property.[4]

The townhouse was located in a prime New York location, with neighbors including the Knickerbocker Club just north at Sixty-second Street; the Pierre Hotel, between Sixtieth and Sixty-first streets; and the Plaza Hotel, two blocks south on Fifty-ninth Street, fronting Grand Army Plaza (the official but almost never used designation for the open squares between Fifth-eighth and Sixtieth streets). The equestrian statue of William Tecumseh Sherman led by the allegorical figure of Victory, created by Augustus Saint-Gaudens (1848–1907), had been installed on the northern end of the square on Memorial Day, 1903. In front of the Plaza Hotel, a large limestone fountain, designed by the architect Thomas Hastings (1860–1929), featured a 1916 statue of the Roman goddess Pomona, by Karl Bitter (1867–1915). It was a perfect location for Gerrie—near art, sculpture, and the cultural and social activities that New York could offer.[5]

When she built the townhouse at 800 Fifth Avenue, Gerrie had elaborate plans for improving its surroundings. She sought to buy up nearby properties, even attempting, unsuccessfully, to purchase the Knickerbocker Club. In 1942 she bought and tore down four residences on adjoining properties at 801–804 Fifth Avenue. And in 1947, she purchased the house just to the east, at 7 East Sixty-first Street, owned by Mrs. Ruth Baker Pratt. At the time, the dwelling was leased and occupied by the Soviet Consulate.

Notoriety surrounded Mrs. Pratt's house while the Soviets occupied it. Soon after World War II, it had been the site of a dramatic incident involving a schoolteacher, Mrs. Oksana Kasenkina, who had been brought to the United States to instruct the children of consular officials. Not wanting to return to her homeland, Kasenkina jumped from a rear, fourth-floor window in an attempt to reach safety and obtain political asylum. She recovered from her injuries and subsequently was granted U.S. citizenship. As well, the building itself became an object of controversy. In the early 1940s, the Russian tenants had significantly altered the interior in order to accommodate their offices, effecting changes that caused the existing elevators, sufficient only for a residence, to be in violation of New York City building codes. When Mrs. Pratt tried to correct this problem, the occupants reportedly padlocked the units and wouldn't allow access—claiming diplomatic immunity. In 1947, around the time Gerrie bought the house, the Soviet Consulate decided to terminate its lease and left the next

A cabinet containing part of Gerrie's bronze collection, Giralda Farms
(Courtesy of the Rockefeller Archive Center)

year. In November 1952, Gerrie had the building razed as part
of her plan to create a lawn and garden around her house.[6]

After her arrival in New York on Tuesday afternoon, Gerrie's
chauffeur would park the car in her townhouse garage, since
she preferred to move around the city by taxi and thereby avoid
parking problems. She came to rely fondly on a particular taxi
driver, establishing a business relationship that continued for
many years. Every week, she would call ahead to let him know
when she was arriving. He would arrange to be with her constantly, taking her wherever she needed to go—even following
her down the street in the taxi as she shopped.[7]

As noted earlier, art and fine-object collecting was a time-
honored hobby, indeed, an avocation, in Gerrie's family. In the
early years of her marriage, she embarked upon what was to

become a perpetual quest for major artworks, especially bronze animal sculpture—not surprising given her love for dogs and, in fact, for all animals. By the early 1920s, she had acquired about 150 works by the French sculptor Antoine-Louis Barye (1796–1875)—featuring so many major examples that it was considered the world's finest collection of that artist's work. Other French sculptors, such as Pierre-Jules Mene (1810–1879) and Rosa Bonheur (1822–1899), also were represented early on, with bronzes of deer, horses, dogs, fowl, and sheep. Eventually, Gerrie came to own more than fifty Bonheur bronzes, as well as a watercolor of *The Horse Fair*. (This was a smaller version of that artist's large 1853–55 oil, purchased by Cornelius Vanderbilt at the A. T. Stewart sale in 1887, which he donated that year to the Metropolitan Museum of Art.) Bronzes by the American sculptress Malvina Hoffman (1887–1966) also were among Gerrie's favorites; she accumulated more than forty.[8]

Gerrie recorded many of her purchases during the 1920s in her diaries. For instance, her entry on January 8, 1929, notes that she attended "the Pulitzer sale" with her secretary Ray Patterson, and that she "bought some bronzes." On March 28, she wrote that she had that day purchased a bronze bust of Benjamin Franklin by Jean-Antoine Houdon.[9]

Gerrie soon decided that her serious interest in collecting would require the services of a competent dealer to guide her acquisitions, to locate various works of art, and to represent her at auctions. In some of her early visits to galleries, she was poorly received; one can only guess that her plain way of dressing—generally in tweeds and sensible shoes—gave the wrong impression to employees of the fashionable establishments on and around Madison Avenue. But James Graham, whose venerable family-owned gallery had been in business since 1857, was different. When Gerrie walked through his door, he greeted her warmly, and Gerrie began a business relationship with the gallery that lasted for about four decades. She was quite fond and highly supportive of the Grahams. During the 1930s, when the Great Depression threatened the establishment's very existence, she

Malvina Hoffman
(American, 1887–1966)
*St. Francis and Animals.*
Bronze, h: 19 in. Signed and indistinctly dated.
Gerrie purchased the statue in 1953
and placed it at the entrance to the
court at Giralda.
(Courtesy of The Morris Museum)

Adolph Alexander Weinman
(American, 1870–1952)
*Abraham Lincoln.*
Bronze, h: 10½ in.
Signed and inscribed: Roma[n]
Bronze Corp, N.Y. and Cellini
Bronze Works, N.Y.
(Courtesy of The Morris Museum)

Cyrus Edwin Dallin
(American, 1861–1944)
*Appeal to the Great Spirit.*
Bronze, h: 21 in.
Signed and dated 1913.
Copyrighted Gorham Co.
(Courtesy of The Morris Museum)

asked what kind of work they thought they could sell most readily in that money-starved climate. "Western bronzes," they replied. Within a short time, a truck pulled up at the gallery containing many examples from her collection, including works by such notable artists as Frederick Remington (1861–1909), to be consigned for sale. Robert Graham, Jr., representing the fifth generation of Grahams to run the gallery, said that as a result of Gerrie's help, his family has long given her credit for saving their business.[10]

James Graham was constantly on the lookout for important paintings, sculpture, and other artifacts on Gerrie's behalf. He tried to have items of interest on hand for each of her visits, to avoid having her go away disappointed. She was fond of Americana, particularly paintings and bronzes of Abraham Lincoln and other important historical figures; this reflected her strong sense of patriotism, despite the fact that she could easily have taken her good fortune to be an American for granted. "Don't forget, it's America first," she would often tell Mary Jane Ellis. "There isn't a country like this one." Ellis further recalled that Gerrie "had a keen sense of history and great pride in our forefathers. She had either a painting or bronze of every man [who] meant anything to this country." She also collected portrayals of Native Americans by major American nineteenth- and twentieth-century sculptors, including James Earle Fraser (1876–1953), A. Phimister Proctor (1862–1950), Charles Russell (1864–1926), and Cyrus Edwin Dallin (1861-1944).[11]

Gerrie came to rely heavily upon Graham, sometimes sending him on acquisition trips. On one notable occasion, she dispatched him to a town in Vermont that owned a bell—installed in a church steeple—that had been cast in the late eighteenth century by Paul Revere (1735–1818). After local officials informed Graham that in order to buy the bell, he would also have to acquire the church, he called Gerrie to see if she would acquiesce to this demand. "Yes," she said. "What do I do with the church?" he asked. "Sell it back to the town for a dollar," she replied. Gerrie got her bell, and the town kept its church.[12]

R. Ward Binks painting at Giralda, about 1935. He is surrounded by some of his 200 portraits of Gerrie's champion dogs. (Courtesy of St. Hubert's Giralda)

Outside the realm of Americana, Gerrie's collecting instincts were rather eclectic. This was due in part to the influence of her family's holdings at Rockwood Hall, her education, and her extensive travels, which stimulated her interest in European fine and decorative arts. Marcy's cousin Helen Hartley Mead Platt believed that Gerrie used experts when necessary but also exhibited good taste and had a systematic way of learning. At times, she would buy in quantity, and often at reasonable prices, since her interests were not necessarily those of mainstream collectors, who often concentrated on a few themes and artists. In time the walls at Giralda were covered with paintings, hung salon-style; display cases were packed with sculpture. Indeed, few surfaces were empty.[13]

A number of those painting-filled walls bore portraits of Gerrie's favorite dogs. In 1931 she commissioned R. Ward Binks (1880–1950), an English painter specializing in animals and particularly in dogs, to come to Giralda to paint portraits of her

R. Ward Binks (English, 1880–1950)
*Jet and Dahalia*
Gouache on paper. 13 x 16½ in. Signed, ca. 1935.
See also original work in photograph of Binks taken
during his extensive stay at Giralda.
(Courtesy of St. Hubert's Giralda)

champions. He ultimately completed more than two hundred
works, concentrating on the German shepherds and English cocker
spaniels. By the time he arrived at Giralda, Binks, then fifty-one,
had had a long and varied career depicting the sporting dogs of
royalty, including those belonging to Britain's King George V at
Sandringham. He also had achieved an international reputation
among animal lovers, traveling to many parts of the world to
complete commissions.[14]

Gerrie's visits to New York would end on Thursday afternoon,
when her chauffeur drove her back to Giralda with her latest
acquisitions. Marcy would always greet her at the door, along
with the entire household staff.

# CHAPTER VII

# LAST YEARS

*Sunset and evening star,*
*And one clear call for me!*
*And may there be no moaning of the bar*
*When I put out to sea.*

—*Crossing the Bar*, Alfred Lord Tennyson, 1889

As she entered her seventies, Gerrie's diary entries consisted almost entirely of single sentences, noting the deaths of friends and family members, with only the occasional mention of an engagement or wedding. On May 11, 1960, she had the sad task of recording the death of her favorite cousin, John D. Rockefeller, Jr. From their earliest years, she and Junior had been great friends, visiting at each other's homes and, as earlier described, sharing a memorable family trip to Alaska in 1899. In later years, although they did not see each other often, they regularly exchanged birthday greetings and invitations.[1]

Junior's first wife, Abby Aldrich Rockefeller, had died in 1948. She had been a most impressive and accomplished woman— not only a major source of strength for her husband but also the driving force behind Rockefeller support for New York's Museum of Modern Art and for the restoration of Colonial Williamsburg.

Abby's death was a loss keenly felt by Junior, whose loneliness led him to remarry in 1951. His new wife was Martha Baird, the widow of a good friend and Brown University classmate. The couple divided their time between their several homes. They spent winters in Tucson.

Marcy also wintered in warmer climates, usually Florida, while Gerrie was content to remain in Madison, planning for upcoming Morris and Essex dog shows and pursuing her interest in art collecting. In 1952 he accepted Junior and Martha's invitation to spend the winter in Arizona. It was a pleasant holiday for Marcy, and while he was there Gerrie sent him a surprise telegram on February 28, his seventy-first birthday. "A thousand thanks for thoughtful telegram. Enjoying Marcellus greatly. We all miss you greatly. Martha and I send affectionate greetings," was Junior's telegraphed response. "These anniversaries have an appalling way of coming too frequently, and it just happens that both his and mine come at a time when so often we cannot be together," answered Gerrie. She went on to write that "it has meant so much to Marcy being with you at Tucson, and he has enjoyed it tremendously. I almost think he is weaned away from Florida. I do appreciate all that you have done for him."[2]

The following year, Junior wrote Marcy imploring both Dodges to visit Tucson, a trip that did not materialize. Also in 1953, he thanked Gerrie for some books and a charming birthday card, which he thought of as a "reminder of wonderful times we have had together on the Alaska trip, horseback riding at Tarrytown and in many other ways in years gone by. . . . [We] still hope that you will both come out here before we turn our faces homeward, that we may welcome you, Ethel, to lovely Tucson, and that we may have the pleasure, Marcellus, with your many other friends here, of seeing you again in an environment with which you are so pleasantly associated in our minds."[3]

Junior's death was not the only loss with which she had to deal. Ray Patterson had died only a few months earlier, on Marcy's seventy-ninth birthday. Ray had been an important employee and a good friend. He had served Gerrie in many capacities—as a chauffeur, as a trusted overseas emissary to purchase dogs for her kennels, as her representative at local municipal hearings and meetings, and as a member of committees established for animal welfare. He had worked hard each year on the Morris and Essex dog show, and he even lived in the mansion at Giralda Farms. Also, it was Ray, of course, who had brought Hartley's body back from France in 1930. Ray's passing left her "terribly upset," recalled her butler Ernest Barton. "'You can't bring him back,' I told her."[4]

Gerrie's weekly visits to New York City grew a little less regular after 1957. In 1958, Mary Jane Ellis began to work for her as a secretary/companion, "a paid daughter," as Ellis characterized the relationship years later. She stayed at Giralda until 1970.[5]

Throughout these later years, religion seemed to play an increasingly important part in Gerrie's life. She had always attended church, especially after Hartley's death, when she found solace in the prayers. On Sundays, the Dodges would usually attend early communion services and then return to Giralda for breakfast. The Reverend William Nieman of Grace Episcopal Church in Madison later noted that "Mrs. Dodge preferred the early service because, as she told me, there's no sermon." He thus acknowledged that she was consistently honest, even when it seemed to hurt a bit.[6]

Her long-standing friendship with Father John Laffey remained important to her. And in March 1961, Pope John XXIII—through his representative the Most Reverend James A. McNulty of New Jersey's Paterson Diocese—recognized her outstanding humanitarian work by bestowing on her the highest honor a non-Catholic can receive from the Church: the Benemerenti Gold Medal. Cited particularly were her generosity to Morristown's All Souls Hospital and the Church of Christ the King in New Vernon, New Jersey, as well as her many other charities. "Many of my prayers have been answered and I have received help many times," she said in accepting the award, "so it is I who have benefited through the great work of the church rather than the church through my offerings."[7]

Despite such honors, Gerrie did not convert to Catholicism, preferring to attend both Grace Church and St. Peter's Episcopal Church, in Morristown, where she particularly admired the organ music. Mary Jane Ellis recalled that Gerrie was well acquainted with Episcopalian as well as Catholic hymns and prayers and that she seemed to derive comfort from services conducted in both faiths. She even built a sanctuary on the estate. Her art collections included several crucifixes, and a large bronze Ming Dynasty Buddha was installed in her garden.[8]

She had outlived her siblings. Her brother William had died in 1922, only five months after their father; and her brother Percy and sister, Emma, had both died in 1934. As she aged, Gerrie came to believe that her health and, consequently, her appearance were "failing," as Ellis described her condition in the early 1960s.

Geraldine Rockefeller Dodge with her German shepherds, ca. 1960. (Courtesy of St. Hubert's Giralda)

She began to turn inward, refusing to entertain relatives and spending more and more time alone in private pursuits, which included an investigation of the Rockefeller genealogy.[9]

In 1962, Gerrie fell and broke her wrist. She was taken to All Souls Hospital in Morristown for treatment. Marcy was concerned about her mental and physical deterioration, as well as about the possibility of further injury (she was later acknowledged to be suffering from the beginning stages of arteriosclerosis, deemed to be chronic, progressive, and irreversible), so he ordered thick carpeting installed in the mansion. Shortly thereafter, she fell again, breaking her hip. When she returned from the hospital this time, she was confined to a wheelchair and could barely speak. She was often confused and unable to handle her affairs.

Marcy began the process of becoming her legal guardian; this was formally accomplished in June 1963. At the same time, his own health was failing, and he knew it. It is possible that he had cancer, but no diagnosis was made public at the time. The Reverend Nieman recalled that Marcy visited Gerrie's room every day—always carrying a little gift for her. But he also realized that his own growing weakness made it likely that he would predecease her. Not long before his death, he told longtime Giralda butler Ernest Barton that he was "afraid Mrs. Dodge is going to outlive me. If so, will you stay with her?" Anxious to be as helpful as possible, Barton replied, "Yes, Mr. Dodge, I will—if I'm allowed to do so."[10]

Marcy soon became bedridden, and now it was Gerrie's turn to visit him daily. The Reverend Nieman remembered that "Mrs. Dodge would come by in the morning and bring him a rose, take it to his bedside, then they would embrace and she would visit for a little bit. Toward the end, he was not able to talk or visit—and she was confused mentally—but she still brought the rose; there was a great deal of affection between them even at the end." Marcy died on Christmas night 1963 of "a long illness," according to the obituary in the Morris County *Daily Record*. Several hundred people attended his funeral service at Madison's Grace Episcopal Church, presided over by the Reverend Nieman. Then began the trip to Sleepy Hollow Cemetery, where Marcy was buried next to young Hartley as he had requested.[11]

It was a great loss to Gerrie, to Marcy's extended family, and to all who knew him. He was well liked by his staff. Mary Jane Ellis recalled his generosity of spirit, and Ernest Barton described him as "one of the finest people I ever encountered," always willing to help with problems and "always able to put himself to your benefit." He had also accomplished a great deal for the community. A *New York Times* editorial recalled former *Times* owner Adolph Ochs's characterization of Marcy as "an outstanding, useful citizen, respected and admired" by all. The writer further noted that Dodge could now be described as "a citizen whose life contributed greatly to the welfare, knowledge and happiness of mankind."[12]

Marcy's philanthropy had never been as well publicized as that of his wife. Nonetheless, he had had an enormous impact with respect to environmental concerns, particularly in Morris County. He made what was perhaps his biggest contribution in the late 1950s and early 1960s, when he almost single-handedly defeated the Port of New York Authority's plan to build a jetport for the metropolitan New York area in New Jersey's Great Swamp, about an hour's drive from Manhattan. Marcy's response to the threat was to purchase more than eighteen hundred acres, much of it from local landowners, and then donate it to the federal government through the North American Wildlife Foundation—with the stipulation that it be left in its primitive state. It was subsequently designated the Great Swamp National Wildlife Refuge. In 1965 a thousand-acre section of the federal preserve was named the M. Hartley Dodge Natural Area by the U.S. Fish and Wildlife Service, in recognition of his generosity.[13]

Marcy's will included many bequests, including gifts to Grace Church, to the Madison-Chatham YMCA, and to area hospitals. He left $2,250,000 to his beloved alma mater, Columbia University. To Gerrie he bequeathed Hartley Farms, cars, horses, jewels, and $100,000.[14]

With Marcy's death, it was necessary that a new guardian be appointed for Gerrie. Morristown attorney Worrall F. Mountain (soon succeeded by Peter C. Netland) and the Fidelity Union Trust Company of Newark were chosen, with Herbert W. Ball designated as Fidelity's administrator. Decisions had to be made concerning her finances, and so the trustees of the William Rockefeller estate (the Chemical Bank New York Trust Company, and James S., William, and Avery Rockefeller, Jr.) petitioned New York Surrogate Joseph A. Cox to rule that Mrs. Dodge be restricted to a yearly allotment of approximately $144,000 for living expenses. They also requested permission to sell her Fifth Avenue residence, asserting that $5 million could be realized from the sale. But Surrogate Cox ruled that the William Rockefeller trust had not been designed to provide Gerrie's only income, since she was already married to an extremely wealthy man when it was established. "[William Rockefeller] was creating trusts," wrote Cox, "to meet the demands of a society which to many would be sheer extravagance but to his family was a habitual way of life." Therefore, limitations would not be placed on Gerrie's living expenses, and no decisions would be made concerning the sale of any of her property while she was still alive. In 1964, Fidelity Union Trust Company asked the Superior Court of New Jersey if it should cut the annual expense of feeding the dogs in her kennels from $50,000 to $14,000, considering that the amount might be too high. But Judge Ward J. Herbert ruled that, given Mrs. Dodge's wealth, the dogs' diet should be maintained at the level to which they had been accustomed.[15]

The courts thus strove to protect Gerrie's way of life as her mental and physical health continued to decline; they also became involved where her art collection was concerned. In better times, she had been wary of fortune seekers and circumspect about the nature of the gifts she bestowed. But in 1960 she made a donation of some of her porcelains to Elmira College, in Elmira, New York, that would lead to a legal wrangle. In recognition of the donation as well as her philanthropic activities and "enthusiasm, energies, and thoughts" concerning the welfare of her community, the college conferred upon her an honorary Doctor of Humane Letters degree. The following year, Gerrie signed a letter of intent and a second letter, prepared on behalf of the college, to donate her entire art collection (then valued at about $1.7 million) to the upstate New York institution but noting that she would "retain possession of them so long as I am able to enjoy them." Another donor had recently given Strathmont, a mansion located seven blocks from the college, to house the artwork.[16]

In 1964, with Marcy no longer alive, Elmira College attempted to take possession of the collection, basing its claim on the letters Gerrie had signed three years earlier. Although her new guardians sued to prevent the institution from succeeding in its claim, in February 1966 Superior Court Judge Ward J. Herbert ruled in favor of the college. That ruling, however, was overturned on

June 20, 1967, by the New Jersey Supreme Court, which determined that Gerrie had been "deteriorating in mental vigor" when she signed away the collection. The opinion, written by Justice John J. Francis, stated that

> *as events proved, she was an open door to the superficial manifestations of friendship and blandishments of able men. She was alone, against the persuasion of three such men who were determined to obtain financial aid for the College from her. The odds were not fair and they became even more unequal when a member of the bar came to their aid in preparing the crucial gift letter which was at odds with the earlier instrument that was "exactly" the kind of agreement she wanted.*

The decision continued with the poignant observation that "the sins of the able are no less sins when committed in what they believe to be a worthy cause." The artwork remained at Giralda Farms and at 800 Fifth Avenue until after her death.[17]

Marcy's desire that Ernest Barton be allowed to stay on at Giralda to care for Gerrie was fulfilled. "It was the saddest thing to see her lying there because she couldn't express herself," the butler recalled. "She knew my voice and she would turn her head towards me and move the lips." It was especially sad, since she had for so many years demonstrated great competence in all of her affairs. Indeed, as Herbert Ball later noted, she had handled business affairs for Giralda, managed the trusts her father created, served as a trustee of the Hartley Dodge Memorial, and kept actively involved in the affairs of St. Hubert's Giralda.[18]

Gerrie's final illness—as mentioned, a form of arteriosclerosis—spanned more than nine years. Round-the-clock nurses attended to her every need, as she stared into the distance, continually declining. Ball arranged to increase the security on the property and had it linked, for the first time, to the Madison police station.[19]

The funeral of Geraldine Rockefeller Dodge, Grace Episcopal Church, August 15, 1973
(Courtesy of the *Madison Eagle* and the Madison Public Library)

Geraldine Rockefeller Dodge died at 1:00 a.m. on August 13, 1973 at the age of 91. Ball later sentimentalized her passing by recalling that his watch stopped at approximately the time of her death, never to run again. He added that the deer on the estate—as if sensing the sadness within the house—massed outside the mansion.

Services were held at Grace Episcopal Church two days later, with the Reverend Nieman officiating. Pointing out that eulogies were not customary in Episcopal Church funerals—and that Mrs. Dodge probably would not have wanted one anyway—Nieman nonetheless was moved to say, "We all know of her gracious and generous help and will always be grateful and remember her good works." Because most of her relatives, friends, and acquaintances were gone, the interment was sparsely attended; only her nephew William Rockefeller, Herbert Ball, and the Reverend Nieman witnessed the ceremony at Sleepy Hollow Cemetery. Her ashes were placed in the Rockefeller family vault. Just outside were the graves of Marcy and Hartley.[20]

# EPILOGUE

> *"The Mission of the Geraldine R. Dodge Foundation is to support and encourage those educational, cultural, social and environmental values that contribute to making our society more humane and our world more livable."*

> —Mission statement, Geraldine R. Dodge Foundation

Geraldine Rockefeller Dodge chose to be remembered after her death as the generous person she was throughout her life. In 1955 she had made a will leaving almost everything to St. Hubert's Giralda. But this was to change, when on October 29, 1962, she executed a new—and final—will. Widespread speculation about how her estate, then valued at some $75–$80 million, would be disbursed was put to rest on September 24, 1973, just over a month after she died, when the contents of this nineteen-page document were made public. Although she made individual bequests to certain friends and employees, she left nothing to her nieces and nephews. She believed that they had been adequately taken care of through her father's estate; in addition, she had relinquished all of her income from the family trust to them in 1950.[1]

The main beneficiary of her final will was to be a new, non-profit corporation—the Geraldine R. Dodge Foundation—created to provide funds for "charitable, scientific, literary or other educational purposes, or for the prevention of cruelty to animals, or for the encouragement of art." The will gave the Foundation latitude to fund a wide variety of projects in areas appropriate to continuing and changing needs and authorized it to "carry out its own programs as an operating and independent organization whenever and to the extent that its Trustees or Directors believe that it can better accomplish its purposes through its own operation rather than through the making of grants or benefits to other existing charitable enterprises." Over the years, the trustees have

accepted this challenge and have taken the initiative to widen
that initial charge by including elementary and secondary education and critical issues affecting the general quality of life. They
also have added foundation-sponsored initiatives, including
the nationally renowned Geraldine R. Dodge Poetry Festival,
a Chinese-language program, and The Principals' Center for
the Garden State. As a result, during its first quarter-century,
under the visionary guidance of its founding executive director,
Scott McVay, it has become one of the major foundations in the
United States.

Given that her final will was made a year after Gerrie signed
"gift" letters to Elmira College concerning her entire art collection
(ultimately ruled invalid by the New Jersey Supreme Court), and
only seven months before the declaration of her incompetence
and the naming of Marcy as her legal guardian, it is likely that he
and, certainly, Ralph Lum, Gerrie's lawyer at the time, provided
appropriate guidance concerning the formation of its provisions.
In light of Marcy's long-standing and well-known support of the
family's philanthropic efforts, it is reasonable to assume that he
would have wanted his wife's estate put to what he considered
the highest purposes.

Shortly after Gerrie's death, it became clear that the courts
would have to settle the issue of the appointment of the will's
executor to administer her estate. The will named Edwin A.
Sayres, Sr., longtime director of St. Hubert's Giralda, and Gerrie's
accountant, Clyde A. Zukswert (who had died in 1965), as co-
executors. But in late August, Sayres's selection was challenged
in court by two of Gerrie's nephews (William A. Rockefeller
and David H. McAlpin), by her guardian (Fidelity Union Trust
Company), and by the New Jersey Attorney General's office (in
its role as representative of a number of charitable institutions).
The challenge included an allegation that Sayres had "violated
a position of trust because he personally profited" from a 1962
sale of land Mrs. Dodge owned in Parsippany-Troy Hills, New
Jersey—an allegation Sayres denied. According to newspaper
reports, in the first round of this legal contest, Superior Court

Judge Robert Muir, Jr., named the Fidelity Union Trust Company
as temporary administrator, citing its familiarity with and constant supervision of Mrs. Dodge's extensive holdings during the
preceding ten years. On March 12, 1974, a final settlement was
reached whereby Fidelity was appointed permanent executor
of the estate. Sayres, meanwhile, became a member of the new
Geraldine R. Dodge Foundation Board of Trustees and was
retained as a consultant to Fidelity with regard to Mrs. Dodge's
charitable intentions. The settlement also included financial
and land donations to St. Hubert's Giralda.[2]

It remained for Fidelity as executor to dispose of Gerrie's
enormous art collection and her two homes, Giralda Farms and
800 Fifth Avenue. But Fidelity recognized that marketing so
much art could cause certain problems. Herbert Ball worried,
for example, that the selling of the great many bronzes of
animals in Gerrie's collection at one time could actually deflate
rather than inflate the market. Nonetheless, the collection had
to be sold, and Sotheby Parke Bernet was chosen to arrange for
and carry out what it dubbed "the sale of the century."[3]

With each day of the auction exhibition in early October
1975, the lines grew longer and longer, with the final count of
those who viewed the collections and toured the house and
grounds of the estate reaching more than sixty thousand people.
Dealers, dog fanciers, collectors, and just plain citizens came to
Giralda. In the barn, a tag sale included books and other items
considered of lesser value, although some rare editions turned
up among those offerings as well.

When the bidding began, it seemed not to follow a pattern,
according to Sotheby Parke Bernet President John Marion, who
regarded it as essentially a celebrity auction. Thus pre-auction
estimates were often low in relation to the prices realized. For
example, a watercolor by Rosa Bonheur that the auction house
had estimated would sell for about $1,200 was bid up to $2,500.
On the other hand, Gerrie's six-foot-tall bronze Ming Dynasty
Buddha, which had been a centerpiece of her garden, sold for only
$9,000 rather than within the estimated $15,000–20,000 range.

Among her household furnishings was a major Kashan rug, featuring eight signature medallions on a red floral ground with palmettes at each corner and a border of cypress trees and roses on a blue ground; it sold for $35,000. There also was a noticeable escalation in the value of some of the furniture. A Louis XV ormolu-mounted marquetry bureau went for $29,000; Gerrie had paid $420 when she bought it in 1929.

Also disposed of in the auction were numerous casts of famous people's hands that had occupied a large display cabinet at Giralda; among them were those of the Polish pianist Ignace Paderewski and of the poets Robert Browning and Elizabeth Barrett Browning. Gerrie's collections of china, silver flatware, and silver hollowware, including many examples made by Tiffany and Company, also were sold. She also had owned bronzes by the American sculptor John Rogers (1829–1904), the original models for his better-known plasters that, in Rogers's day, had adorned thousands of homes. Of these bronzes, *The Referee*, which the auction house had estimated would sell in the $1,000–$1,500 range, went for $20,000. Rogers's *School Examination*, also carrying the same initial estimate, brought $19,000 from the same buyer.

Sold at fairly reasonable prices (within the estimate range) were thirty-eight works by Malvina Hoffman (1885–1966), an important American sculptress, the majority from a 1930 commission from the Field Museum in Chicago to document the physical characteristics of various peoples for that institution's Hall of Man.

Animalier bronzes by Antoine-Louis Barye, Pierre-Jules Mene, Isador Bonheur (1827–1901), Auguste-Nicholas Cain (1822–1894), and other important European sculptors sold well. And when Sotheby's held a special sale for Gerrie's major collection of Baryes in New York later in October, the total realized was about twice the expected amount. Indeed, Barye became a feature of the art market that year. American western as well as historical bronzes also did well. A study by John Quincy Adams Ward (1830–1910) for his full-length statue of George Washington sold for $3,000.

*The Passing of the Buffalo* by Cyrus Edwin Dallin (1861–1929),
which Gerrie had commissioned in 1931 for the grounds of
Giralda, was estimated to sell for $15,000 to $20,000. When the
hammer finally came down, the price had reached $120,000.
Gerrie would have been astonished and thrilled at the auction
records set after her death. And as it turned out, the effects of
a glut on the market that Herbert Ball had feared simply did
not materialize.

The sale of Gerrie's collection of jewelry and marble sculpture
also made news that fall. In New York on October 15, a 26.6-carat
diamond pendant sold for $425,000. Additionally, four pieces of
jewelry set with rare pigeon blood rubies went for $690,000,
double their pre-sale estimate. On November 29, a British collector
purchased her marble bust of Benjamin Franklin by Jean-Antoine
Houdon for $310,000—at the time the highest price ever paid
for a work by that French sculptor. Knowing that the bust would
surely be taken to England, Gerrie's longtime dealer, James Graham,
expressed great disappointment. "With all the millions in this
country, how could we let it go?" he asked, after bidding on it
for a client who, if successful, intended to present it to the White
House as a U.S. Bicentennial gift. Graham had sold it to Gerrie
in 1939, for $5,500.[4]

After the auctions were over, the Woman's Association of
Morristown Memorial Hospital asked the Fidelity Union Trust
Company for permission to use Giralda Farms for its 1976 Mansion
in May, a major interior-design fund-raiser held to benefit the
hospital. Recognizing that Mrs. Dodge had been generous to
Morristown Memorial during her lifetime, Fidelity agreed. It was
clear to all parties involved that the mystique of the mansion
and estate would help the worthy cause of the hospital. Ernest
Barton remembered that the monthlong event, held in the "show-
house of the century," drew about fifty-five thousand attendees,
including First Lady Betty Ford and Jacqueline Kennedy Onassis.
More than $270,000 was raised.[5]

It also was time to dispose of her homes and property. In
Madison, Giralda Farms had grown to more than 370 acres—

part in Madison and part in Chatham Township. Local planners wanted to see it preserved intact. The New Jersey College of Medicine and Dentistry reportedly was interested for a while, but nothing came of it. Some were moved to suggest that Giralda be used for a county park, but Gerrie had asserted in her will that she wanted it to remain on the tax rolls, for the benefit of the two communities in which the land was located. Ultimately, Giralda was sold to the Prudential Insurance Company for about $9 million for the development of an office park. Although the mansion was torn down, some of the outbuildings remain and are still in use. The grounds, which Gerrie had cared for so lovingly, are still beautiful, and, in honor of the Dodges, the property retains the name Giralda Farms.[6]

Today the legacy of Geraldine Rockefeller Dodge and Giralda continues. In 1998 the Foundation funded publication of *Always with Us*, a collection of accounts about the fifty-one Madison men who lost their lives in World War II and in the Korean and Vietnam wars. The book was written and compiled by the Madison War Memorial Committee, headed by Madison's present mayor, John J. Dunne. To celebrate the publication, Schering-Plough, the international pharmaceutical company now headquartered at Giralda Farms, hosted an event for more than two hundred relatives of the men in *Always with Us*. Mayor Dunne observed that through the book, Mrs. Dodge had again served Madison by making a posthumous gift in honor of some of its citizens. He also found it fitting that the celebration was taking place on her property.[7]

At this writing, plans are under way to revive the Morris and Essex Kennel Club Dog Show: it will be held on October 5, 2000, on the grounds of Giralda Farms, thereby ending a forty-three-year dormancy. C. Freeman Ayers, president of the revived club, reports that in memory of Geraldine Rockefeller Dodge, the club intends to hold a dog show there every five years.[8]

Gerrie's most significant legacy remains the Foundation bearing her name. Its trustees met for the first time on July 19, 1974, filed a certificate of incorporation that October, and began grant

making on October 7, 1975, with an endowment of $62.6 million.
The charter trustees, after consulting with philanthropists, elected
officials, and local citizens, established the Foundation's five major
areas of giving: education, the arts, critical issues, animal welfare,
and Morris County projects; these remain its main focus today.

In the ensuing quarter-century, the Foundation has given
$200 million in grants to a variety of organizations and programs
in these five areas. About thirty percent has gone to education,
another thirty percent to critical issues. The arts have received
about twenty percent, with animal welfare receiving ten percent.
The remaining ten percent has gone to fund projects in Morris
County and other programs outside the major categories. One
of these is the biennial Geraldine R. Dodge Poetry Festival, which
attracts thousands of teachers and students for several days of
immersion in the hearing and enjoyment of poetry—surely
an event that Gerrie, given her interest in poetry, would have
enjoyed. As the new millennium opened, the Foundation's net
assets stood at $355 million, a firm base from which to carry
Gerrie's philanthropic spirit well into the future.[9]

How should Geraldine R. Dodge be remembered? She was
the little girl, caring for her first terrier, who grew up to be the
"dog fancier of the century" and "the first lady of dogdom." She
was a child of the Gilded Age, surrounded by wealth and fine
art, who matured into a knowledgeable collector. And she was
the optimistic wife and mother—tempered by family tragedy—
who became a major philanthropist, turning her great loss into
an enduring civic memorial and a foundation that continues
to benefit us all.

Photograph of Geraldine Rockefeller Dodge, about 1940

# NOTES

*Abbreviations*

**AR**  Almira Rockefeller

**HWB**  Herbert W. Ball

**DR**  *Daily Record* (Morris County, New Jersey)

**GR**  Geraldine Rockefeller

**GRD**  Geraldine Rockefeller Dodge

**JDR**  John D. Rockefeller, Sr.

**JDR, Jr.**  John D. Rockefeller, Jr.

**ME**  *Madison Eagle* (Madison, New Jersey)

**MHS**  Madison (New Jersey) Historical Society

**MJE**  Mary Jane Ellis

**NEN**  *Newark Evening News*

**NSN**  *Newark Sunday News*

**NYHT**  *New York Herald Tribune*

**NYT**  *New York Times*

**SL**  *Star Ledger* (Newark, New Jersey)

**WR**  William Rockefeller

**WRP**  William Rockefeller Papers, Rockefeller Archive Center, North Tarrytown, New York

**YD**  *The Youngest Daughter*, videotape produced by the Madison Public Library in conjunction with the Fairleigh Dickinson University Instructional Media Center, Madison, New Jersey. Executive producers: Nancy Singleton, Ursula Sommer, and Elizabeth Budell. Produced by Barry Byrne and Edna Ierley. Interviews conducted between 1975 and 1978.

CHAPTER I

EARLY LIFE

1. For comments by John Marion, President, Sotheby Parke Bernet, Inc., and Herbert W. Ball, an officer of the Fidelity Union Trust Company, before the Giralda Farms sale, see interviews October 8 and 16, 1975, YD.

2. HWB interviews, October 8 and 16, 1975, YD; MJE interviews, July 20 and December 7, 1977, YD; Ernest Barton interview, March 1, 1977, YD. Barton was employed as the Dodges' butler in June 1937 and continued working at the estate until July 1976. In his interview, he reported that he had previously worked for the British royal family at Windsor Castle and then for Arthur Curtiss James.

3. For information regarding the wealth of Morris County millionaires in the late nineteenth century, see John W. Rae and John W. Rae, Jr., *Morristown's Forgotten Past: "The Gilded Age"* (Morristown, N.J.: Mark Lithographers, 1979), esp. Chap. 3, "The Millionaires: Who They Were," 24–41. See also Larry Bataille, "Historic Hartley Farms," *Country Roads* 4, no. 1 (spring 1993): 46; Charles E. Surdam and William Gardner Osgoodby, *Beautiful Homes of Morris County and Northern New Jersey* (Morristown, N.J.: Pierson and Surdam, ca. 1910); Marjorie Kaschewski, *The Quiet Millionaires* (Morristown, N.J.: Morris County's Daily Record, 1970); John Foreman and Robbe Pierce Stimson, *The Vanderbilts and the Gilded Age: Architectural Aspirations, 1879–1901* (New York: St. Martin's Press, 1991), esp. Chap. 5, "Florham," 103–25; and John T. Cunningham, *Images of America: Madison* (Dover, N.H.: Arcadia Publishing Co., 1998).

4. Mark Twain and Charles Dudley
Warner, *The Gilded Age* (Hartford and
Chicago: American Publishing Co.,
1873); L. Marx Renzulli interview,
December 22, 1977, YD; and Andrew
Carnegie, "The Gospel of Wealth"
(repr., Bedford, Mass: Applewood
Books, 1998; originally published in
*North American Review* [June and
December 1889]).

5. In France, the name is Roquefeuil and
variants; in Germany, Rockefelter and
variants. See Ron Chernow, *Titan: The
Life of John D. Rockefeller, Sr.* (New
York: Random House, 1998), 3; and
Rockefeller Genealogy, WRP. Diell was
also known as Thiel or Diel, among
other spellings.

6. Chernow, *Titan*, 6–9. George Davison
died on December 13, 1777. It is not
known whether battle wounds or dis-
ease caused his death. In addition to
Lucy (1838–1878), John D. (1839–1937),
and William (1841–1922), William
and Eliza Rockefeller's children were
Mary Ann (1843–1925), and the twins,
Franklin (1845–1917), and Frances
(1845–1847).

7. For information on the double life
of William Avery Rockefeller, see
Chernow, *Titan*, 57–59, 462–65.

8. Ibid., 125.

9. For discussions of Rockefeller philan-
thropy, see Allan Nevins, *John D.
Rockefeller: The Heroic Age of
American Enterprise*, 2 vols. (New York:
Charles Scribner's Sons, 1940); and
Chernow, *Titan*. See also
"Philanthropies of Rockefellers Total
More Than $780,000,000," NYHT,
July 16, 1933. In 1891 Senior hired
Frederick T. Gates to handle the
Rockefeller philanthropy. But by the
late 1890s, Junior began sharing that
responsibility and gradually took
charge. See Nevins, *John D. Rockefeller*,
2: 288–90.

10. For an account of William Rockefeller's
rise in the oil business, see Nevins,
*John D. Rockefeller*, vol. 1. See also
William O. Inglis interviews with John
D. Rockefeller 1917–20, JDR Papers,
Rockefeller Archive Center.

11. The six men who collectively invested
$1 million to establish Standard Oil
were Samuel Andrews, Henry M.
Flagler, Stephen V. Harkness, Oliver
Burr Jennings, John D. Rockefeller, and
William Rockefeller. See Nevins, *John
D. Rockefeller*, vols. 1 and 2. See also
William Rockefeller Family Scrapbooks,
WRP. I am grateful to Laura and George
Levy for their help in documenting the
career of William Rockefeller.

12. Almira Rockefeller was born in New
York City on March 19, 1844. Her
family lived briefly in Elmira, New
York, before settling in Cleveland.
In 1912 and 1913, the U.S. House
of Representatives Committee on
Banking and Currency, popularly
known as the Pujo Committee, inves-
tigated what it considered to be
monopolistic practices by Standard
Oil. William Rockefeller, who had been
suffering from chronic throat problems,
began to testify, but because of his illness, he was excused from the obliga-
tion. William's corporate directorships
included: the Rutland Railroad Co.;
the Anaconda Copper Mining Co.; the
Consolidated Gas Co.; the New York
Central Railroad and nearly all of its
subsidiaries; the Lackawanna and
Western Railroad Co.; the Northern
Pacific, Chicago, Milwaukee and St.
Paul Railway Co.; the Brooklyn Union
Gas Co.; the Delaware, Lackawanna
and Western Railroad Co.; the
Mechanics' National Bank; Mutual Life
Insurance Co; National City Bank;
Hanover National Bank and the U.S.
Trust Co. See William Rockefeller
obituary, NYT (clipping, WRP).

13. William ultimately amassed some four hundred acres in Greenwich. Eventually, his son William G. took over the house at One Elm and enlarged it, while Percy built a new house on the portion of the property he was given. Both houses were razed in the 1930s. I am grateful to Laura and George Levy for providing background on the William Rockefeller holdings in Greenwich.

14. William and Almira Rockefeller's six children were: Louis Edward (March 2, 1865–August 3, 1866), Emma (June 8, 1868–August 11, 1934), William Goodsell (May 31, 1870–November 30, 1922), John Davison II (March 8, 1872–June 10, 1877), Percy Avery (February 27, 1878–September 25, 1934), and Ethel Geraldine (April 3, 1882–August 13, 1973). The name Ethel was not included on her New York City birth certificate (no. 335561), indicating that she may have acquired it at some later time. By the end of her teens, she dropped it in favor of Geraldine or Gerrie, but her parents continued calling her Ethel. Her birth certificate mistakenly listed the family's address as 681 Fifth Avenue. On July 7, 1932, this clerical error was finally corrected.

15. For a history of the growth of Manhattan in the nineteenth century, see Ric Burns and James Sanders, *New York: An Illustrated History* (New York: Alfred A. Knopf, 1999), esp. Chap. 2, "Order and Disorder," 68–137, and Chap. 3, "Sunshine and Shadow, 1865–1898," 138–215. See also Mary Dillon Edmondson, *Profiles in Leadership: A History of the Spence School, 1892–1992* (West Kennebunk, Maine: Phoenix Publishing, 1991), 3.

16. Burns and Sanders, *New York*, 101. St. Thomas Church was founded in 1823. For a general architectural history for this period, see William H. Jordy and William H. Pierson, Jr., *American Buildings and Their Architects*, 4 vols. (New York: Doubleday, 1972). After 689 Fifth Avenue was demolished, in 1926, the Aeolian piano showroom occupied the site. Today both 689 and 691 Fifth Avenue are contained within the Elizabeth Arden building.

17. John D. Rockefeller and his family remained in Cleveland after William moved to New York, but within a relatively short time, they began making regular trips to the East. In 1884 they purchased a home at 4 West Fifty-fourth Street in New York City. For a history of Kykuit, see Ann Rockefeller Roberts, *The Rockefeller Family Home: Kykuit* (New York: Abbeville Press, 1998).

18. Harold G. Gulliver, "Rockwood Hall on the Hudson," *Country Life* (March 1923): 7–10 (clipping, WRP). As a young man—before accumulating a fortune primarily in railroads—Arthur Curtiss James (1867–1941) worked for Phelps, Dodge and Company. His father, Daniel Willis James, was a vice-president of that firm. Marcellus Hartley Dodge's grandfather William Earl Dodge had co-founded the company in 1833 with his father-in-law, Anson G. Phelps.

19. See "Rockwood Hall: The Country Estate of the Late William Rockefeller," 1922, real estate brochure published by William A. White, 46 Cedar Street, New York, WRP. After William died in 1922, the estate was put on the market, but it did not sell. Subsequently, a group of investors (Rockwood Hall, Inc.) took it over and established an exclusive country club by obtaining operating capital from the sale of 450 acres of the estate to John D. Rockefeller, Jr. In 1928 Rockwood Hall, Inc. also secured a $625,000 loan from

the Equitable Trust Company of New
York. By 1937, after the country club
operation failed, Junior purchased
the remaining land and buildings and
leased them to the Washington Irving
Country Club, then to a theater operation, neither of which was successful.
Thereafter, Junior found the upkeep of
the massive house to be so expensive
that, in 1942, he had it demolished.
Four years later, he deeded the property
to his son Laurence, who continues
to lease it to the State of New York as
a public park for $1 a year; he also
underwrites the maintenance cost. In
1970 he sold 80 acres of the property
to IBM for its world trade center. For
more on the history of the area and
its population, see "Rockwood Hall:
Historical Background," typescript
prepared by the State of New York
Department of Parks and Conservation,
n.d., WRP. For Biltmore, see Susan M.
Ward and Michael K. Smith, eds.,
*Biltmore Estate: A National Historic
Landmark* (Asheville, N.C.: Biltmore
Company, 1989).

20. "Westchester Today," unidentified
Yonkers, N.Y., newspaper clipping,
February 17, 1962, WRP.

21. MJE interviews, July 20 and December
7, 1977, YD. At age twenty, Gerrie
won a blue ribbon riding her horse
Tendresse at the Westchester Horse
Show, WRP. The total appraised value
of the contents of Rockwood Hall after
William's death was $109,635.95. See
"Rockwood Inventory and Appraisal,"
by Henry Brady, Auctioneer and
Appraiser, 139 West Thirty-third
Street, New York, June 24, 1922, WRP.

22. See *A. T. Stewart Collection of Paintings,
Sculptures and Other Objects of Art*
(New York: American Art Association,
1887). For a report on the sale of this
collection at Chickering Hall (Fifth
Avenue and Eighteenth Street, New

York), see *New York World*, March 25,
1887. The sale is reported to have
grossed $270,625. William Rockefeller
paid $15,250 for the Nicol painting
and $3,050 for the Hart.

23. For a history of the school, today
known as the Spence School, see
Edmondson, *Profiles in Leadership*.
After Brearly and Spence were
established, the next two progressive
schools to open in New York were
Chapin (in 1901) and the Nightingale-
Bamford School (in 1920).

24. Edmondson, *Profiles in Leadership*, 10.

25. Letters from AR to Emma Rockefeller,
February 28 and March 5, 1895, WRP.
In her diary Gerrie documented two
additional grand tours of Europe she
took at ages fourteen and fifteen. On
May 20, 1896, she sailed on the *St. Paul*
with her parents and brother Percy for
a three-month trip to England and the
Continent that ended on August 29.
On June 30, 1897, John D. Rockefeller,
Jr., joined Gerrie and her family on
the *Paris* for a two-month European
summer vacation. The party returned
on August 21.

26. GR diary, January 9, 14, and 28, 1899,
January 20, 1900, WRP. See also "Music
Heard Yesterday. 'Lohengrin' given at
the Metropolitan Opera House Before
a Very Large Audience," NYT, January
10, 1899.

27. "Over the Continent to Alaska:
Vacation with Rockefeller," August 6,
1899, unidentified newspaper clipping,
WRP; GR diary, May 27, 1899 and
January 11, 1900. In the latter, she
notes her visit to Pocantico Hills for a
family reunion after the trip. See also
letter from Junior to Gerrie, December
30, 1953, in which he reminds her of
the "wonderful times we have had
together on the Alaska trip," WRP. She
also may have been inclined to drop
the name Ethel in favor of Geraldine

after reading "Geraldine, Strong with
the Spear," identifying "Geraldine" as
"superior in historic distinction." See
typescript, WRP.

28. GR diary, April 3, 1901, WRP. There
was undoubtedly more description
included, but the diary page is missing.

29. Ibid., May 23–28, 1901, WRP.

30. Ibid., June and July 1901, WRP. For a
description of Bay Pond, see *New York
Daily Tribune*, July 6, 1899, WRP.

31. For an account of the "adoption" of
Caroline North by the Rockefellers, see
"The Poor Girl Who Has Become Miss
Rockefeller's Chum," *World Magazine*,
August 28, 1904 (clipping, WRP); and
GRD diary, February 20–March 14,
1902. Gerrie and Caroline Woodruff
North remained lifelong friends.

32. GR diary, March 28–April 27, 1903.

33. Ibid., April 28–July 30, 1903.

34. James M. Barrie, *Sentimental Tommy:
The Story of His Boyhood* (New York,
Charles Scribner's Sons, 1896); idem,
*The Little White Bird, or Adventures
in Kensington Gardens* (London:
Hodder and Stoughton, 1902); Henryk
Sienkiewicz, *Quo Vadis* (Boston: Little
Brown and Company, 1897); Émile
Zola, *Rome* (London: Chatto and
Windus, 1896).

35. GR diary, May 12–December 22, 1904,
WRP.

36. Ibid., February 7–November 3, 1905,
WRP.

37. Ibid., November 23, 1905, and January
13–June 6, 1906, WRP. One of the
two extant portraits is owned by the
borough of Madison and hangs in the
municipal building's council chambers.
The other is owned by The Morris
Museum (see page 6 and front cover).



# CHAPTER II

MARCELLUS HARTLEY DODGE

1. GRD scrapbooks, WRP.

2. GR diary, October 6–November 18,
1906, WRP.

3. GR diary, 1901–6, WRP. Laura and
George Levy, authors of a forthcoming
biography of William Rockefeller,
believe they have identified a pattern
whereby Rockefeller family members
appeared to acknowledge their engage-
ments by entering capitalized initials
of their intended spouses in their
diaries. If that is the case, it is possible
that Geraldine Rockefeller and
Marcellus Hartley Dodge were engaged
on November 18, 1906. It is also interesting to note that in Gerrie's diary
entry for November 18, 1907, exactly
a year later, she refers to "our anniver-
sary dinner." The Frelinghuysens
were married on February 7, 1907.

4. GR diary, January 18–February 12,
1907, WRP.

5. I am grateful to Nicolas W. Platt and
Helen Hartley Mead Platt, relatives of
Marcellus Hartley Dodge, for providing
information on the Dodge genealogy.
For a biography of William Earl Dodge,
see *The National Cyclopaedia of
American Biography* (New York: James
T. White and Co., 1891–1907), 3: 174.

6. For Marcellus Hartley, see Alden
Hatch, *Remington Arms: An American
History* (New York and Toronto:
Rinehart and Co., 1956). For additional
biographical information, see also
"Sudden Death of Marcellus Hartley,"
obituary and editorial, NYT, January 9,
1902; and Hartley Family Genealogy,
WRP. Emma Hartley (August 16,
1858–March 2, 1881) was the eldest
daughter of Marcellus and Frances
Hartley. The younger daughters were
twins, Grace and Helen (b. August 16,

1860). Grace Hartley Stokes died on April 2, 1896, and Helen Hartley Jenkins died on April 24, 1934.

7. Hatch, *Remington Arms*, Chap. 14, 98–104.

8. "Sudden Death of Marcellus Hartley," obituary, NYT, January 9, 1902; Columbia University Alumni Federation Office; Hatch, *Remington Arms*, 128; "Marcellus Hartley Dodge," obituary, NYT, December 26, 1963; "Vacation Home at Convent," ME, September 2, 1904. See also Burns and Sanders, *New York*, 88, where the authors quote the "Tenement House Report," written by the philanthropist Robert M. Hartley in 1853: "Crazy old buildings—crowded rear tenements in filthy yards; dark damp basements; leaky garrets, shops, outhouses, and stables converted to dwellings, though scarcely fit to shelter brutes—are the habitations of thousands of fellow citizens in this wealthy city."

9. Hatch, *Remington Arms*, 209; Dodge NYT obituary, December 26, 1963.

10. See Meyer Berger, *The Story of the New York Times* (New York: Simon and Schuster, 1951); and "Book Reveals Aid Given to 'Times' by M. H. Dodge," ME, October 18, 1951. See also Susan E. Tifft and Alex S. Jones, *The Trust: The Private and Powerful Family behind the New York Times* (Boston, New York, and London: Little, Brown & Co., 1999), 76, where the authors report that Ochs repaid the loan after Mrs. Dodge mentioned her husband's "distress" after the recently collapsed Russian government had repudiated its contract for the purchase of rifles from Remington Arms.

11. I am grateful to the Columbia University Federation Office for providing this information. See also "Name Columbia Building for Mr. Dodge," ME, August 5, 1965. Marcy also was the co-donor to Columbia of 335 autographed letters by the English art critic, essayist, and reformer John Ruskin (1819–1900).

12. Engagement announcement, NYT, March 19, 1907; wedding announcement, NYT, April 19, 1907. The state of New York Dodge marriage certificate (no. 10298) identifies Gerrie as "Ethel Geraldine Rockefeller" and lists Marcellus Hartley Dodge's occupation as "merchant." William Rockefeller and Barent Lefferts (Dodge's best man) served as witnesses. See also "Rockefeller-Dodge Wedding Marked by Charm, Simplicity and Dignity," *Daily News*, Tarrytown, New York, August 29, 1960.

13. GRD diary, June 23 and July 4, 1907.

14. Ibid., August 14–September 13, 1907.

15. Author interview with Helen Hartley Mead Platt, December 6, 1999. Honeymoon Cottage, also known as Two Shoes, burned down in 1950. It was vacant at the time but had recently been occupied by Richard Swift, general manager of the Columbia Broadcasting Company. See "Two Firemen Injured When Dodge Estate House Burns," ME, February 9, 1950. For information concerning the building of 691 Fifth Avenue, see William Rockefeller diary, January 17, 1910 ("Spent some time with Ethel & Architect on plans for 691 Fifth Avenue"); January 21, 1910 ("Consulted with Mr. Ehoun about plans for 691"); and June 12, 1911 ("Lunched with Ethel at 691"). Thus by June 1911, Marcy and Ethel (as her father was still calling her) had moved into the house.

16. Hatch, *Remington Arms*, 213-214.

17. GRD diary, May 8, 1915, WRP.

18. Hatch, *Remington Arms*, 222.

19. Ibid., 223.

20. Ibid. Despite the difficult situation he was in, it appears that Marcy managed to bolster his finances significantly as a result of having liquidated his hold-

ings in Midvale Steel and Ordnance in 1915. See "Marcellus H. Dodge Cleans up $24,000,000 on 'War Bride'," ME, November 12, 1915.

21. For a brief history of Madison, see "The Model Borough: Madison, One of New Jersey's Most Picturesque, Healthful and Progressive Towns," ME, March 19, 1897. See also Cunningham, *Images of America: Madison.*

22. To date, the meaning of the name Onunda has not been determined. In addition to his businesses, James had interests in mining and transportation, among other private investments. He reportedly left an estate of more than $26 million. For the donation of James Park, see "James Park Dedicated: Presented to the Borough of Madison by D. Willis James on the Fourth Day of July, 1898," ME, July 8, 1898. For a contemporaneous article on the library, see "Madison Library Building: Another Munificent Gift to the Borough from Mr. and Mrs. D. Willis James—a Full and Complete Description," ME, January 27, 1899. After the borough constructed a new library in 1968, James's building was sold to the Museum of Early Trades and Crafts. In 1997, with partial funding provided by the New Jersey Historic Trust, the museum restored the building, giving it an appearance near that of the original Brigham and Adden design and interiors.

23. The Dodges reportedly paid about $750,000 for the estate. See ME, September 13, 1907, and May 5, 1916, for articles about D. Willis James and his wife, Ellen Stebbins James, after they died. See also "Beautiful James Estate Is Sold to Marcellus Hartley Dodge," ME, July 14, 1916. According to Mary Jane Ellis, Gerrie sold her jewelry to purchase the James estate; when William Rockefeller learned of this, he reportedly repurchased the jewelry and returned it to his daughter (author interview, October 11, 1999). See also "Dodge Estate Opened," ME, June 1, 1917. Author interviews with Helen Hartley Mead Platt, December 6, 1999, and January 15, 2000. At the time the Dodges purchased his parents' estate, Arthur Curtiss James was president of the Curtiss Securities Company and vice-president of Phelps, Dodge and Company, the firm established in 1833 by William Earl Dodge (Marcellus Hartley Dodge's grandfather) and his father-in-law, Anson Phelps.

24. The purchase of the Dunham-Harkness estate added seventy-five acres. See "Dunham Land Is Purchased," ME, March 29, 1929. See also "Lovell Estate Sold to Mrs. M.H. Dodge," ME, May 27, 1932; this added another forty acres.

25. Author interview with MJE, October 11, 1999.

26. Beginning in 1896, the William Rockefellers spent winters on Jekyll Island, Georgia, a warm-weather haven favored by wealthy industrialists. In 1899 they purchased Indian Mound, a home named for a hill in front of the property that contained oyster shells but that originally was thought to be filled with Indian bones. See William Barton McCash and June Hall McCash, *The Jekyll Island Club: Southern Haven for America's Millionaires* (Athens and London: University of Georgia Press, 1989); and June Hall McCash, *The Jekyll Island Cottage Colony* (Athens and London: University of Georgia Press, 1998). See also letter from WR to GRD, January 9, 1919, WRP.

27. Letters from AR to GRD, November 17, 1918; February 3 and March 4, 1919; January 14, 1920, WRP.

28. WR diary, January 9–17, 1920; GRD diary, January 23, 1920, WRP.

29. Letter from William G. Rockefeller to GRD, March 5, 1922, WRP. See also WR diary, June 12–15, 1922, WRP. The

reburial service for William, Almira,
and William G. Rockefeller in the completed family crypt at Sleepy Hollow
Cemetery was held on December 13,
1922.

30. "Rockefeller Will Filed for Probate
Yesterday," ME, June 30, 1922. See
also "William Rockefeller's Estate
Appraised at $67,647,660 Net," ME,
August 17, 1923. The gross value of the
estate was set at $102,584,438. Each of
the four Rockefeller children alive at
the time of William's death was to
receive one-quarter of the net estate, or
$14,372,149, in trust, with the principal
to go to their children. See also letter
from GRD to her nephew William
Rockefeller, May 21, 1951.


CHAPTER III

MARCELLUS HARTLEY DODGE, JR.

1.  Letter from AR to GRD, July 1, 1914, WRP.
2.  Grace Hartley Mead and Helen Hartley
Mead Platt interviews, May 26 and
October 21, 1976, YD.  William
McAlpin graduated from Princeton in
1926 and John D. Rockefeller III in
1929. David H. McAlpin II had graduated in 1902, and D. Hunter McAlpin
(Hartley's maternal uncle) in 1885.
3.  "M. Hartley Dodge Jr. Killed in Auto
Accident in France Last Friday," ME,
September 5, 1930.
4.  Ibid. See also "Delightful Qualities
of Hartley Dodge Are Recalled by
Eisenhart at Exercises," ME, May 31,
1935 (Eisenhart speech at the dedication of the Hartley Dodge Memorial);
and Grace Hartley Mead and Helen
Hartley Mead Platt interviews, May 26
and October 21, 1976, YD.
5.  Alumni Records and Archives offices,
Princeton University; "Marcellus H.
Dodge, Jr. on Princeton Newspaper

Board," ME, June 24, 1927. See also
GRD diary, 1929–30, WRP.
6.  "M. H. Dodge, Jr. in New Yacht on Five
Week Cruise," ME, August 9, 1929.
Some confusion remains as to whether
Gerrie was in agreement with the
decision to purchase a car for Hartley.
The Reverend William Nieman later
recalled that either Marcy or a friend
of Marcy's gave the car to Hartley for
graduation and that Gerrie blamed this
gift for her son's death. See Nieman
interview, May 12, 1976, YD.
7.  GRD diary, July 20, 1930, WRP. See
also "M. Hartley Dodge Jr. Killed," ME,
September 5, 1930, and the editorial
in the same issue, in which the writer
describes Hartley's good character
and sincerity.
8.  See article in *La France de Bordeaux et
du Sud-Ouest*, August 30, 1930, which
clearly identifies Hartley as the driver
of the car when the fatal accident
occurred. I am grateful to Nicolas W.
Platt and Megan Smyth of Burson-
Marsteller for securing this report
from *Direction des Archives
Départementales de la Gironde*, in
order to clear up the long-standing
confusion about this question. Ralph
W. Applegate, who lived until 1976,
spent most of his life after the tragedy
in Chicago. He served in the U.S. Army
during World War II. See photograph
of Applegate and his wife on the occasion of his promotion to the rank of
major, *Chicago Daily News*, n.d., WRP.
9.  Emma Rockefeller McAlpin diary,
August 30, 1930, WRP.
10. GRD diary, August 29, 1930, WRP.
11. "M. Hartley Dodge Jr. Buried in Family
Plot with Military Honors," ME,
September 12, 1930.
12. For documentation of the burial of
Hartley on September 11, 1930, see
Sleepy Hollow Cemetery Register of
Interments, January 1, 1900–December

31, 1930, Sleepy Hollow Cemetery, Sleepy Hollow, New York. Over the years, unfounded accounts and rumors have spread regarding Gerrie's reaction to her son's death and to the date of his burial. For example, Clarice Stasz in *The Rockefeller Women* (New York: St. Martin's Press, 1995), 295, makes the claim that Gerrie refused to bury Hartley, becoming so "unhinged that she kept the coffin with her son's remains in her drawing room for weeks." There is no documentation for this allegation, and it is untrue. See also Robert Woolley, *Going Once: A Memoir of Art, Society and Charity* (New York: Simon and Schuster, 1995), 97, where Hartley's death is declared to be a suicide by "a very morose young man," another undocumented and false assertion. In fact, all available evidence clearly indicates that Hartley was an intelligent, friendly, and popular young man with a bright future. Woolley also mistakenly describes Gerrie as "living in a time warp," a somber woman dressed in black who never got over her son's death and lived as a recluse after 1936. As the present biography documents, after Hartley died, Gerrie did manage to go on with her life, continuing her outstanding philanthropy (much of which was done in her son's memory), hosting dog shows every year for thousands of people, collecting art, and managing her extensive estate.

13. GRD diary, November 12–December 13, 1930, WRP.

14. MJE interviews, July 20 and December 7, 1977, YD; author interview with MJE, October 11, 1999.

15. Author interviews with Helen Hartley Mead Platt, December 6, 1999, and MJE, October 11, 1999.

16. MJE interviews, July 20 and December 7, 1977, YD.

17. Ibid.



# CHAPTER IV

"THE DOG FANCIER OF THE CENTURY"

1. Author interviews with Meg Strubel, vice-president of St. Hubert's Giralda, November 10 and 22, 1999.

2. See, for example, "The First Lady of Dogdom," *Country Roads* 4, no. 1 (spring 1993): 32–37, 82.

3. J. Allen Boone, *Kinship with All Life* (New York, Evanston and London: Harper and Row, 1954).

4. "Dog Owned by Mrs. Dodge Takes Prizes for Finest Breed," ME, October 13, 1922; "World's Best Shepherd Dogs Are Exhibited Here," ME, May 30, 1924; and "Mrs. Dodge to Be Judge, Not Exhibitor, at Show," ME, February 4, 1943. See also "Long Interest in Dogs Prompted Mrs. Dodge to Establish Kennels," ME, June 26, 1931. Mrs. Dodge sent Raymond L. Patterson as well as A. McClure Halley in search of dogs. See "Raymond Patterson Sails for Germany," ME, March 29, 1929.

5. "Giralda Kennels Has Best Bred Dog in United States," ME, April 24, 1925.

6. HWB interviews, October 8 and 16, 1975, YD.

7. *Dogdom*, April 1924, clipping, "Morris and Essex Shows" scrapbook, Collection of St. Hubert's Giralda, Madison, New Jersey.

8. "Mrs. Dodge Is Hostess to the Maharajah of Jind," ME, August 1, 1924; MJE interviews, July 20 and December 7, 1977, YD. See also "Giralda Farm's Kerry Triumphs in Spaniel Show at New York. Rippel Family Also Cops Ribbons," ME, January 9, 1947.

9. Geraldine Rockefeller Dodge, *The English Cocker Spaniel in America* (New York: Approved by the English Cocker Spaniel Club in America, 1942); Geraldine Rockefeller Dodge and

Josephine Z. Rine, *The German Shepherd Dog in America* (New York: Orange Judd Publishing Co., 1956).

10. The other portion of the laboratory at Cornell University College of Veterinary Medicine is the Nancy Sayles Day Division, established by Colonel and Mrs. Lee Garnett-Day. See "Giralda Division for Canine Health Begun at Cornell," ME, June 8, 1950. I am grateful to Jeanne Griffith (Assistant Director of Communications and Marketing at Cornell's College of Veterinary Medicine), Dr. Douglas McGregor (Associate Dean for Research and Graduate Education in the College of Veterinary Medicine and former director of the Baker Institute), and Dr. Leland Carmichael (Professor of Virology, Emeritus) for providing information about the James A. Baker Institute for Animal Health (named in honor of Baker, its founder, after his death in 1975). Gerrie's nephew William Rockefeller served on the Baker Institute Advisory Council.

11. "Shepherd Exhibit to Be Held in May," NYT, March 18, 1924; "Shepherd Clubs to Gather Here in Convention," NYHT, May 11, 1924; "Merits of Shepherd Are Expounded in Educational Talks," NYHT, May 24, 1924; Frank F. Dole, "Morris and Essex Kennel Club Show Promises to Be Success," NYHT, May 8, 1927; "Morris-Essex Bench Show Huge Success," ME, June 3, 1927.

12. "Madison, Mrs. Dodge's Debtor," ME, June 7, 1929. See "Morris and Essex Dog Show Dates Are Fixed," ME, April 18, 1930, an article announcing that von Stephanitz will be coming to judge. Mrs. Dodge owned an English translation of von Stephanitz's *Der Deutsche Schaferhund in Wort und Bild* (The German Shepherd in Word and Pictures) (Munich: Verein für deutsche Schaferhunde, S.V., 1925). See also

Edwin J. Sayres, Sr., interviews, October 8, 1975, and May 13, 1976, YD; and "Dunham [Harkness] Land Is Purchased," ME, March 29, 1929. Sayres, Sr., reported that he had known Gerrie since 1932, when he and his family were professional dog handlers and competed against her in dog shows.

13. "Record Entry for Dog Show," ME, May 15, 1931; "See You at Madison," ME, May 22, 1936; "40,000 Spectators Break All Records at Giralda Fixture," ME, May 29, 1936; "World's Greatest Dog Show Breaks Records Saturday," ME, June 1, 1939; "Mrs. Dodge Adds 20 Acres to Dog Show Parking Lot," ME, May 14, 1953.

14. "World's Largest Dog Show Will Be Resumed This Year; Thirty Breeds among Entries," ME, November 22, 1945; "Morris and Essex Dog Extravaganza Ready for Saturday," ME, May 23, 1946; "35,000 Attracted to Giralda Farms for Revived Show," ME, May 29, 1946.

15. Ernest Barton interview, March 1, 1977, YD.

16. "No Dog Show for Next Year," ME, October 9, 1958.

17. "Tale of a Dog Named 'Sam' Has Happy End," ME, December 15, 1966.

18. "Dog's Patron Saint Invoked Locally," ME, September 4, 1958; Edwin J. Sayres, Sr., interviews, Oct. 8, 1975 and May 13, 1976, YD. In 1982 Edwin J. Sayres, Jr., took over the presidency of St. Hubert's Giralda, and Edwin J. Sayres, Sr., remained on the board until 1991. Elizabeth McCorkle is the current president.

19. "Mrs. Dodge Gives Borough New Kennel for Dog Pound," ME, March 17, 1955. See also "No Dog Show for Next Year," ME, October 9, 1958.

20. "Mrs. Dodge Gets Double Honors," ME, February 16, 1950; "GRD Named

Dogdom's Woman of the Year by the Gaines Research Center," ME, February 15, 1951; "Mrs. G.R. Dodge Receives Award," ME, February 22, 1951; "Quaker Oats Company to Honor Mrs. Dodge," ME, May 22, 1951; "Giralda Farms Awarded 'Fido,'" ME, February 18, 1954.


CHAPTER V

PHILANTHROPY

1. "Hand-Wrought Brochure to Mrs. Dodge Is with Privately Cherished Things," ME, June 7, 1935; "A Magnificent Memorial," ME, May 31, 1935. For the full text of *Adonais*, see Donald H. Reiman and Sharon B. Powers, eds., *Shelley's Poetry and Prose* (New York: W. W. Norton, 1977), 388–406.
2. Attributed to Geraldine Rockefeller Dodge, GRD scrapbooks, WRP.
3. "Large Gift Made Memorial Hospital," ME, February 6, 1920; "Generosity of Mrs. Dodge Aids Memorial Hospital," ME, March 4, 1921; "Gift from Mrs. Dodge Aids Student Nurses," ME, March 11, 1921; "Dodge Prize for Nurses Awarded at Memorial," ME, June 2, 1921. In the early 1940s, she also donated a building to Overlook Hospital in Summit, New Jersey, which the hospital named Hartley House, at her request. See "Name House at Hospital in Honor of Mrs. Dodge," ME, July 30, 1942.
4. "Mrs. M. H. Dodge Presents Pumping Engine to Madison," ME, July 30, 1920; "New Motor Fire Engine the Gift of Mrs. Dodge," ME, May 13, 1921; "Mrs. Dodge's Generosity," editorial, ME, May 13, 1921; "Mrs. Geraldine R. Dodge Formally Presents Engine," ME, May 20, 1921; "All Madison Celebrates Biggest Day in History," ME, May 20, 1921; "Presentation of Engine Draws Many to Madison," NEN, May 14, 1921; "Mrs. Hartley Dodge Makes up New Fire Apparatus Deficit," ME, August 4, 1949; "Mrs. Dodge Gives Borough $16,000 for New Pumper," ME, January 1, 1953.
5. "Mrs. Dodge Buys on Greenwood Ave.," ME, July 14, 1922; "Mrs. Dodge Would Build New Church" and "The Bethel Church Matter," editorial, ME, November 17, 1922; "Mrs. Dodge Makes Gift to Borough," ME, August 17, 1923; "Mrs. Dodge Thanked for Playground," ME, September 14, 1923; "Playground to Be Completed," ME, October 5, 1923.
6. "The Taxpayer's Forum: Madison's Generous Benefactor Writes Open Letter Complaining of Grudges and Petty Politics above Community Advantages," and "Mrs. Dodge's Letter," editorial, ME, September 14, 1923; "Tomorrow is Madison's Play Day," ME, June 20, 1924; editorial, "The Dodge Field," ME August 8, 1924. According to Ted Monica, former football coach and athletic director of Madison High School, in the 1930s Mrs. Dodge's generosity to the borough led the school to name its athletic teams the Dodgers.
7. "Mrs. Dodge Donates Nets," ME, June 26, 1925; "Mrs. Dodge to Sponsor Tent Caterpillar Drive," ME, March 23, 1928. In addition, in 1926, after lightning struck and caused an explosion at the U.S. Navy arsenal at Lake Denmark near Mt. Hope, N.J., she sent money to provide medical as well as other aid to the injured. See "Noble Generosity," ME, July 16, 1926.
8. "Miller Property Sold: Mrs. Dodge the Purchaser," ME, March 4, 1921; "Mrs. Marcellus H. Dodge to Sue on Smith Option," ME, April 8, 1921; "Mrs. Dodge Gets Title to Kings Road Property," ME, January 13, 1922;

"Council Thanks Mrs. Dodge for Interest in Boro," ME, January 20, 1922; "To Turn Lot at Kings Road and Green Ave. into Park," ME, May 12, 1922; "Mrs. Dodge Presents Land for Public Use," ME, September 16, 1927; and "A Splendid Gift," editorial, ME, September 16, 1927. See also "Niece of Rockefeller Gives $50,000 Site to Madison, N.J.," NYT, September 15, 1927.

9. "Dodges Donate Memorial to Son's School," ME, July 3, 1931.

10. "Dodge Memorial Municipal Building Planned for Opposite the Madison D.L.&W. Station," ME, December 18, 1931.

11. "Dodge Building Plans Are Begun," ME, December 4, 1931; "Dodge Structure Plans Acclaimed by Madisonians," ME, December 25, 1931; Shapter also had created the plan for the athletic field Gerrie gave the borough in 1924. According to Mary Jane Ellis, the weather vane atop the Hartley Dodge Memorial is based on one Gerrie saw en route to a dog show in Wellesley, Massachusetts. She located the artist and had him replicate it. See MJE interviews, July 20 and December 7, 1977, YD.

12. "Endowment Completed," editorial, ME, January 10, 1936.

13. "Start Excavating for Site of New Borough Building," ME, September 16, 1932; "Ordinance to Pave Way for Erection of Dodge Building," ME, August 12, 1932. Drawn up by Henry G. Pilch, the borough attorney, in conference with Albert H. Holland, Mrs. Dodge's official legal representative, it reads: "An ordinance giving Geraldine R. Dodge full and complete authority and permission to enter upon and take possession of certain lands owned by the borough of Madison, for the purpose of erecting a municipal building thereon to be known as the Hartley Dodge Memorial." See also "Award Contract for Municipal Building to Crawford's Firm," ME, September 23, 1932; and "Contractor Starts Work on Municipal Building Monday," ME, October 28, 1932.

14. Steelworkers were brought in from Newark who, after finishing work on the municipal building, returned to construct the framing on the new post office in that city. The Joseph Hall-Smith Company of New York was hired for the electrical work; John E. Joyce of Newark for the plumbing; and Meneely and Company of Watervliet, New York, furnished the bell for the bell tower. See "Splendid Public Spirit," editorial, ME, February 26, 1932; "Dodge Estate Work Brings Jobs to Unemployed," ME, March 25, 1932; "A Protection against the Cold," editorial, ME, November 18, 1932; "Sixty Men Working on Dodge Building," ME, April 28, 1933; "Completing Steel on Dodge Building," ME, February 3, 1933; and "100 Men Employed on Dodge Building," ME, September 1, 1933. The Dodges also arranged to buy and deliver large quantities of firewood and other supplies to the needy during this period. See "Wood and Food Is Given to Indigent," ME, February 19, 1932.

15. "Dodge Memorial Presented to Borough Hailed Unique among Public Buildings," and "Invocation Address Given By Fr. Laffey," ME, May 31, 1935; "Hartley Dodge Memorial Building Presented to Madison," ME, June 7, 1935. The building's rotunda contains bronze plaques documenting the dates of groundbreaking (September 13, 1932), start of construction (October 26, 1932), and building dedication (May 30, 1935), as well as one that bears a profile of Hartley, after the 1926 marble by the sculptress Beatrice Longman (see page 90.).

16. "Firemen Honor the Donor of the Building," ME, July 19, 1935; "Mr. Dodge Wins $10 by Sliding down Pole," ME, July 19, 1935; "Firemen to Be Guests of Mr. and Mrs. Dodge," ME, April 3, 1936.

17. "Tribute to Memory of M. Hartley Dodge, Jr.," ME, July 30, 1936. Beginning in 1936, whenever July 29 fell on a weekend, the flowers were sent to Giralda instead.

18. "Sprinkler System Partly Completed," ME, August 17, 1939; "Mrs. Dodge Gives Air Cooling Units to Borough Hall," ME, August 16, 1956; "Portrait of Donor of Hartley Dodge Memorial Unveiled," ME, June 16, 1938; "Mrs. Dodge Makes Gifts to Boro Hall," ME, February 24, 1938. For a brief biography of Friedrich August von Kaulbach, see E. Bénézit, *Dictionnaire Critique et Documentaire des Peintres, Sculpteurs, Dessinateurs et Graveurs* (Librairie Gründ, 1966), 5: 222.

19. "Mrs. Dodge Presents Historic Paintings and Busts to Borough," ME, May 14, 1942; "A Gracious Lady," editorial, ME, May 14, 1942; "Lincoln Portrait Cleaned and Restored by Experts," ME, November 5, 1942. See also "They Meet in Splendor: Council Room Is Enhanced by Great Art," ME, August 23, 1962. On the Travers portrait, see Harold Holzer, "Some Contemporary Paintings of Abraham Lincoln," *The Magazine Antiques* 107, no. 2 (February 1975), 314–22. See also John J. Dunne et al., *Always with Us* (Morristown, N.J.: The Print Shop, 1998). Besides her gifts to the Hartley Dodge Memorial municipal building, in 1942 Gerrie donated books to the Madison Public Library. See "Mrs. H. M. (sic) Dodge Gives over Sixty Books to Library," ME, October 8, 1942; "Mrs. Dodge Gives Library Her Book [*The English Cocker Spaniel in America*]: Library Also Presented with Story of John D. Rockefeller," ME, October 29, 1942.

20. "Mrs. Dodge Honored by Community Leaders at Dinner Monday Night," ME, April 20, 1950; "This Citizen Loves Madison," editorial, ME, April 20, 1950; "Mayor Describes Dodge Testimonial in City Magazine," ME, July 20, 1950; "Leading Citizens Honored," ME, April 23, 1953.

21. "Water Tower Site is Given by Mrs. Dodge," ME, July 27, 1950; "Mrs. Dodge Gives Lackawanna Site for New YMCA," ME, December 11, 1958; "Mrs. Dodge OK's Ground for Corps," ME, August 17, 1961. The generosity related to honoring her son's memory was not limited to Madison. For example, she donated the M. Hartley Dodge Memorial Lodge to the Morris-Sussex Area Council of the Boy Scouts of America at Allamuchy, New Jersey. See "Boy Scouts Honor Mr. and Mrs. Dodge," ME, June 22, 1950; and "Mr. and Mrs. Dodge at Allamuchy Dedication," ME, June 29, 1950.

22. "Plan Ceremony to Mark Dodge Land Donation," ME, October 7, 1948.

23. Reverend William Nieman interview, May 12, 1976, YD.

24. Recollection by Scott McVay, January 1, 2000; MJE interviews, July 20 and December 7, 1977, YD; author interview with MJE, October 11, 1999.

25. Letters from Ernest Johnson to GRD, October 3 and 15, 1951; letters from GRD to Ernest Johnson, October 8 and 19, 1951, WRP; MJE interviews, July 20 and December 7, 1977, YD.

CHAPTER VI

ART

1.  MJE interviews, July 20 and December 7, 1977, YD.
2.  Ibid.
3.  Mary Jane Ellis recalled that Gerrie had definite ideas about the handling of the family trust and her investments. She believed that sixty percent of one's savings should be put in bonds and forty percent placed in stocks. See MJE interviews, July 20 and December 7, 1977, YD.
4.  "Five Story Home in Fifth Avenue, N.Y. for Mrs. Dodge," ME, December 7, 1923.
5.  See Joseph Lederer, *All Around the Town: A Walking Guide to Outdoor Sculpture in New York City* (New York: Charles Scribner's Sons, 1975).
6.  "Wreckers Tear down Four Houses for Mrs. Dodge," ME, Sept. 10, 1942. See also "Millionaire Row: A Relic Remains," NYT, February 3, 1964; and Peter Hellman, "The Mystery House at 61st and Fifth," *New York*, October 11, 1971, 35-38. For additional newspaper clippings concerning 800 Fifth Avenue, see GRD Scrapbooks, WRP.
7.  According to Mary Jane Ellis, Gerrie bought the medallion for her taxi driver's cab; thus he was understandably devoted to her. Letter from MJE to the author, November 17, 1999.
8.  *Dogdom*, April 1924, clipping, WRP. See also Leo Lerman, *The Museum: 100 Years and the Metropolitan Museum of Art* (New York: Viking, 1963). For a sense of the scope of Geraldine Rockefeller Dodge's holdings, see "The Contents of Giralda" and the seven additional auction catalogues published to advertise and sell her collection, October 11, 1975–May 14, 1976.
9.  See GRD diary, January 8 and March 28, 1929. She eventually donated Houdon's bust of Benjamin Franklin to the borough of Madison as part of a large gift of artwork for its council chambers. See "Mrs. Dodge Presents Historic Paintings and Busts to Borough," ME, May 14, 1942.
10.  Author telephone interview with Robert Graham, Jr., November 16, 1999.
11.  Letter from GRD to MJE, February 21, 1956; MJE interviews, July 20 and December 7, 1977, YD.
12.  Author telephone interview with Robert Graham, Jr., November 16, 1999; MJE interviews, July 20 and December 7, 1977, YD.
13.  Author interview with Helen Hartley Mead Platt, December 6, 1999.
14.  See William Secord, *R. Ward Binks (1880–1950)*, exh. cat. (New York: William Secord Gallery, Inc., 1990).


CHAPTER VII

LAST YEARS

1.  GRD diary, May 11, 1960, WRP.
2.  Telegram from JDR, Jr., to GRD, February 28, 1952; letter from GRD to JDR, Jr., March 7, 1952, WRP.
3.  Letter from JDR, Jr., to MHD, January 12, 1953; letter from JDR, Jr., to GRD, December 30, 1953, WRP.
4.  See, for example, "Patterson Host to County Radio Members, Guests," ME, February 17, 1949; "Committee Named in Effort to Solve Stray Dog Problem," ME, July 26, 1945; and Ernest Barton interview, March 1, 1977, YD.
5.  MJE interviews, July 20 and December 7, 1977, YD.
6.  Reverend William Nieman interview, May 12, 1976, YD.
7.  "Gets Papal Medal: Mrs. Dodge, Episcopalian, Honored," NSN, March 26, 1961; "Bishop Presents Gold Medal to Mrs. G. Dodge," ME, March 30, 1961.

8. MJE interviews, July 20 and December 7, 1977, YD.

9. Agnes L. Scholder, who worked in the Rockefeller office at the Lincoln Building, 60 East Forty-second Street, New York, assisted her with the genealogy.

10. Reverend William Nieman interview, May 12, 1976, YD; and Ernest Barton interview, March 1, 1977, YD

11. Reverend William Nieman interview, May 12, 1976, YD; "M. Hartley Dodge Dies; Finance, Charity Leader," DR, December 26, 1963; "Marcellus Hartley Dodge Dies: Ex-Remington Arms Chairman," NYT, December 26, 1963; "M. H. Dodge Service Is Attended by 300," NYT, December 29, 1963; "Hoover, Ike Join in Dodge Tribute," NEN, December 29, 1963; "Many Attend Rites for Famous Man," ME, January 2, 1964. Marcellus Hartley Dodge's death certificate lists his cause of death as "Renal Failure–Uremia." According to Helen Hartley Mead Platt, New York Governor Nelson Rockefeller met Marcy's funeral procession to Sleepy Hollow Cemetery at the state border. Rockefeller also attended the interment service.

12. "Dodge Will Benefits Many Local People and Agencies," ME, January 23, 1964; "An Outstanding Citizen," editorial, NYT, December 28, 1963. See also Ernest Barton interview, March 1, 1977; and MJE interviews, July 20 and December 7, 1977, YD.

13. See Kenneth Haynes, "'Marcy' Dodge, Man of Special Distinction," ME, January 2, 1964; and "Dodge Memorial: Wildlife Area Will Bear His Name," NEN, December 27, 1965.

14. See Last Will and Testament of Marcellus Hartley Dodge and two codicils, June 1 and December 1, 1963.

15. "Mrs. Dodge Given New Guardian," ME, January 16, 1964; "Rules on Mrs. Dodge's Dogs," NEN, June 24, 1964; "Seems a Rich Pooch Needn't Mooch," *New York Daily News*, June 25, 1964; "Dodge Canines Get the Best," ME, July 9, 1964; "Bank to Set Dodge Income," ME, January 21, 1965.

16. "Elmira College Honors Mrs. Dodge," ME, July 7, 1960; "Elmira College Sues for Dodge Art Gift," DR, July 30, 1964; "Guardians of Mrs. Dodge in Art Collection Dispute," NEN, December 9, 1964.

17. "Elmira College Wins Fight over Mrs. Dodge's Art," DR, February 8, 1966; "College Gets Dodge Art," NEN, February 8, 1966; "Mrs. Dodge's Art Going to College," ME, February 17, 1966; "Court Rules Dodge Art Stays Put," ME, June 22, 1967; "Court Voids Widow's Art Bequest," SL, June 2, 1967. Gerrie's guardians were represented by Emory C. Risley. Donald B. Kipp represented the college. The chairman of Elmira College's board of trustees at the time of the "gift" was Harold MacGraw, a former Madison resident. For the text of the Supreme Court of New Jersey's opinion see, *In the Matter of Geraldine R. Dodge, An Alleged Mental Incompetent. Elmira College, Plaintiff-Respondent, v. Fidelity Union Trust Company, et al., 50* N.J. Reports (1967) at p. 192 et seq.

18. Ernest Barton interview, March 1, 1977; HWB interviews, October 8 and 16, 1975, YD.

19. HWB interviews, October 8 and 16, 1975, YD.

20. "Madison Mentor Leaves Legacy of Love to Area," ME, August 16, 1973; "Mrs. M. Hartley Dodge Dies," DR, August 14, 1973; "Geraldine Rockefeller Dodge, Founder of Kennel Club, Dead," NYT, August 14, 1973; "Mrs. Ethel Dodge: American Aristocrat," DR, August 14, 1973; "Private Burial to Follow Services for

Mrs. Dodge," DR, August 15, 1973; "Service Simple for Mrs. Dodge," DR, August 16, 1973; HWB interviews, October 8 and 16, 1975, YD. Geraldine R. Dodge's death certificate indicates that her body was cremated. Her immediate cause of death is listed as cerebrovascular thrombosis due to general arteriosclerosis. Other significant conditions noted are diabetes mellitus and pyelonephritis.

## EPILOGUE

1. See Last Will and Testament of Geraldine Rockefeller Dodge, October 29, 1962. See also letter from GRD to her nephew William Rockefeller, December 26, 1950, relinquishing all income from the family trust to her nieces and nephews, WRP.

2. See "Dodge Will Drama," DR, August 19, 1973; "Fidelity Bank Retains Dodge Trust Reins," DR, August 24, 1973; and "Dodge $85 million Left to Foundation," NYT, September 25, 1973. In January 1974, the 1962 will was challenged in court by St. Hubert's Giralda, which had been named as the main beneficiary of the 1955 will. See "Dodge Competency," DR, January 6, 1974; "New Roadblock for Dodge Settlement," ME, January 10, 1974; "Dodge Will Fight Settled; Bank Administers Estate," DR, March 13, 1974; and "What's Ahead for Dodge Land Now That Will Is Settled?" ME, March 21, 1974. See also "Joint Report of Settlement Negotiations," Superior Court of New Jersey Chancery Division, Morris County, docket no. P-29-72.

3. "Thousands See Hints of Past They Never Knew," NYT, October 7, 1975; "Giralda: Beginning of the End," ME, October 9, 1975; HWB interviews, October 8 and 16, 1975, YD; John Marion interview, October 8, 1975, YD. See also Sotheby Parke Bernet auction catalogues for the Geraldine Rockefeller Dodge Sales, October 11, 1975–May 14, 1976. St. Hubert's Giralda and the Geraldine R. Dodge Foundation each received some of the Dodge artwork. The foundation subsequently gave a grant to the Morris Museum to furnish a room in Mrs. Dodge's memory containing several pieces, including a portrait of her by Friedrich August von Kaulbach, painted in 1906 (see page 6 and cover).

4. "A Bust of Franklin Is Sold for $310,000," NYT, November 30, 1975.

5. Even during the almost ten-year period of incompetence that preceded her death, Gerrie's guardians continued to make regular donations to the hospital in her name. See Morristown Memorial Health Foundation: Donations from Geraldine Rockefeller Dodge, January 1, 1958–August 13, 1973; "Mansion in May '76 Comes to Dodge Estate," DR, November 9, 1975; Shirley Friedman, "Many Decorators Have Designs on Giralda Farms Mansion," SL, February 23, 1976; and Ernest Barton interview, March 1, 1977, YD.

6. Kenneth Haynes, "Can You Picture the Dodge Estate as a County Park?" ME, May 14, 1970; "What's to Become of the Giralda Farms Property?" ME, August 30, 1973; Kenneth Haynes, "Putting off the Inevitable," ME, October 4, 1978.

7. See Dunne et al., *Always with Us.*

8. Author telephone interview with C. Freeman Ayers, January 13, 2000.

9. See 1999 Annual Report, Geraldine R. Dodge Foundation.